GOD IN GREEK PHILOSOPHY

PUBLISHED WITH THE AID OF
THE CHARLES PHELPS TAFT MEMORIAL FUND
AND THE GRADUATE SCHOOL

GOD IN GREEK PHILOSOPHY

TO

THE TIME OF SOCRATES

BY

ROY KENNETH HACK, B. LITT. (OXON.)

*Professor of Classics, Fellow of the Graduate School,
University of Cincinnati*

PRINCETON: PRINCETON UNIVERSITY PRESS
FOR THE UNIVERSITY OF CINCINNATI

FOREWORD

THE Department of Classics at the University of Cincinnati reissues this book, which has been out of print for many years, in the belief that it remains a valuable work in its original form and ought to be available to those who want it. The reprinting is made possible by financial support from the Classics Fund, a gift of Louise Taft Semple in memory of her father, Charles Phelps Taft.

Those of us who knew and studied with Professor Hack think of him with personal affection and with admiration for his learning, his vigor and courage, and his stimulating guidance. His death in 1944, at the age of sixty, was a painful loss to us.

We are well aware, as he was, that many of his contemporaries disagreed with his conclusions about Greek religion and early Greek philosophy. If he himself were offering the book today one may be sure that he would have taken note, in his own mind at least, of the new work and criticism that have been made known in the interval of forty years. Yet the central thought in his understanding of the problems would presumably not have changed in essence from that which he presented with clarity and precision in 1931. It was based not upon analysis of interpretations by others but upon the surviving texts of the Greek authors, which change but little. In the present generation many students of the subject will disagree again with Hack's conclusions. They cannot properly do so, however, without stretching their minds in hard clear thought. This is what he would have wanted.

J. L. Caskey

Cincinnati
March 1969

PREFACE

[handwritten annotation: Hack II Cornford, Jaeger: stresses continuity between Hesiod, Homer and Presocratics, who are as much religious as scientific.]

THIS sketch of the doctrines of the supreme divine power in pre-Socratic philosophy was undertaken as the result of some studies in the origin of the Stoic doctrines of God and Pneuma (the Spirit of God), which were published in *Ricerche Religiose* (1926-1929). In those studies, the conclusion was reached that it was extremely difficult, if not impossible, to explain the preoccupation of Greek philosophers, from Plato to Zeno, with the problem of the true nature of the supreme divine power, if that problem had first been raised by Plato. In the nineteenth century, many scholars believed that the history of Greek philosophy presented us with a picture of two groups of philosophers, between whose activities there was scarcely any relation: the pre-Socratic philosophers were supposed to have expended their best energies upon the investigation of nature, and to have created natural science; Plato and Aristotle were supposed to have subordinated natural science to metaphysics, and to have created the science of the supreme divine reality. The activities of the first group were supposed to have culminated in the complete "materialism" of the Atomists. Furthermore, it was generally held that the first group had broken resolutely away from earlier Greek thought and traditions about the nature of divine power. In a period of less than three centuries, the main current of Greek thought was believed to have changed its direction twice.

It therefore seemed necessary to reexamine the sources; and this work is based throughout upon the Greek texts, both primary and secondary. When allowances are made for the distortion inevitable in reporting the thought of others, the evidence of the sources indicates, I believe, that the continuity

[vii]

PREFACE

of Greek thought about the supreme god was never really broken. At any rate, it is possible to explain the available evidence, if the pre-Socratic philosophers were attempting to improve the definition of the nature of the supreme divine power; if on the other hand they were attempting first of all to found natural science, the succession of their doctrines becomes unintelligible, much of the available evidence must be discarded, and the interest which Plato and Aristotle manifest in divine reality will appear to be a sudden and more or less miraculous development. I have translated a considerable part of the evidence, in the hope that a reader who does not know Greek may be able to judge, although imperfectly, for himself; and it has been possible to restore the reading of the original MSS. in a number of passages where emendation was justified only by a preconceived theory of what the author should have written.

I gratefully acknowledge my profound obligation to Zeller, whose monumental *Philosophie der Griechen* is the foundation of all modern work in this field, because of Zeller's thoroughgoing integrity and of his immense erudition, over which he had attained complete mastery; and to Diels, whose collection of the *Fragmente der Vorsokratiker* is an indispensable instrument and the product of the finest scholarship. Burnet's *Early Greek Philosophy* and Robin's *La pensée grecque* are valuable and independent works; and I have named, in a select bibliography, some of the other scholars whose investigations have added to our knowledge of this period. The *Griechische Religionsphilosophie* of Otto Gilbert, the *From Religion to Philosophy* of F. M. Cornford, and the *Cycle mystique* of A. Diès are especially important for the study of early Greek philosophy.

In addition, it seems to me that all who deal with the philosophy of this or of any period are, or should be, under the greatest obligations to Bergson. Bergson, whose infinitely painstaking researches into the relations between thought and expression, into the genesis of philosophical schools and the

PREFACE

war of philosophical sects, and into the meaning of negative judgments, have revolutionized the discipline of the history of philosophy, is undergoing the usual experience of a prophet. A large part of contemporary thought is already twenty years behind the times, so far as the work of Bergson is concerned; and while it is inevitable that there should be a great deal of misrepresentation and misunderstanding of the achievement of any genius, it should be possible to lessen the arrogance and the futility of those petty quarrels which enslave philosophy to science and hinder the growth of human liberty.

To the genuinely liberal foundation of the Graduate School of this University, to the Board of Directors of this University, to the Dean of the Graduate School, Professor L. T. More, and to the Chairman of the Department of Classics, Professor W. T. Semple, I am especially indebted for their sympathetic aid and support; and I am under great obligations to Professors Ernesto Buonaiuti of the University of Rome, George La Piana of Harvard University, and Allen West of the University of Cincinnati, for their most friendly help and criticism.

I am glad also to acknowledge the generous aid given, toward the expenses of publication, by the Charles Phelps Taft Memorial Fund.

R. K. HACK.

Cincinnati
May 19, 1930.

CONTENTS

CHAPTER I

GOD AND THE GREEK PHILOSOPHERS

THALES of Miletus, commonly known as the first philosopher in this western world, said that Water was the cause and source of all things. He also said that all things were full of "gods," and were alive. What did Thales and his followers mean? What transformations did this belief that the substance of the universe is divine undergo during the first great creative period of Greek philosophical thought? What happens when philosophers attempt to deal with the idea of divinity? The experience of the Greeks does not of course afford a complete answer to this last question, but it will at least give us some instructive hints. The best of Greek thought is still living, but through our own negligence, and through the excessive specialization of modern scholarship, it is living a life that is much too quiet and retired. Hence philosophers are able to startle the modern world by announcing a theory which really belongs, very often, to the fourth century B.C. Hence, very often, the histories of Greek science and philosophy and religion have tried to separate by inflexible definitions facts which are really interdependent.

The views of Thales and his followers are a case in point. Some historians are certain that rational science is the source of true philosophy and the one genuine identifying mark by which it can be recognized; therefore they reject with horror the suggestion that various cosmogonies or stories about the origin of the universe can be the germ from which Greek philosophy developed. The fact that Thales and the rest of the Ionians attribute divinity to the world or to the primary substance is more or less of a stumbling-block, but they get over it by affirming that when the Ionians use the term "god" they mean something wholly secular and non-religious. Other historians who are equally good scholars and deal with precisely the same facts insist that the Ionians constantly operate with religious ideas, although they are inspired by a scientific and practical impulse which, we are told, culminates in the doctrine of the atomists, with life and growth, god and the soul, completely banished from the universe. It is obvious that the real difference between these conflicting views concerns the date at which Ionian thought may be said to have become secular and scientific; the school of Burnet holds that divinity had been pretty effectively removed from the Ionian scheme of the world long before the time of Thales, while Cornford holds that the process was not finished until some time in the fifth century B.C.

We shall see later that there is some reason to believe that divinity was never effectively banished from the Ionian scheme of the world. In fact, divinity in philosophical systems resembles nature in the lines of Horace: *tamen usque recurret*—it will always find a way back no matter how hard you try to expel it. The Ionians, however, may be an exception. If it is true that their civilization was utterly secular, then Thales may have meant something quite non-religious by his use of the term "god," and the most brilliant chapter in the history of early philosophy may turn out to be really a chapter in the history of science, a strange and hostile prelude to the profoundly religious systems of Plato, Zeno, and Epicurus. The meaning of "god" (θεός) is therefore not a mere question of translation, but is the point at which a problem involving the whole history of Greek thought is concentrated. And since the words which Thales used were a social product, and must have been more or less comprehensible to his fellow-Ionians, we must inquire what educated Greeks of his time (Thales flourished about 585 B.C.)

thought about the gods and the universe, and to what extent their notion of divinity was non-religious.

Fortunately, this inquiry, which is already sufficiently difficult, need not be complicated by the question of origins. For this purpose, the literary evidence is alone important, since it alone proves actual usage; and it makes no difference whether Zeus was originally a flint fetish, or Apollo a sprig of ivy, unless the influence of those origins is definitely present in the sixth century B.C. Homer is of course our first and greatest witness, and in some ways the most inaccessible. It is clear enough why he is our greatest witness; his genius immortalized his poems, and there was no Greek who knew not Homer. It was perhaps less clear that Homer is not easy of access. Greek is still known to some scholars; there are plenty of copies of Homer, and translations abound. What then bars the way to Homer?

CHAPTER II

HOMER

THERE is one adequate explanation of the inaccessibility of Homer, and that is his genius. It is not merely that he, like the other greatest poets, does not abide our question, but has a breadth and depth of creative power beneath which he hides all that is narrowly and eccentrically personal. His popularity is also a result of his genius, and his popularity has brought upon him, like an army in search of plunder, the commentators. The result is that the poet has almost disappeared. The critics of the nineteenth century were particularly industrious, and they obscured or denied the evidence of Homer in the name of every possible preconceived theory. The "material" provided by his poems was treated as if it were a coral-bed, or a sedimentary deposit of centuries of poetical activity (the phrase belongs to the eminent historian Eduard Meyer), from which facts could be arbitrarily selected and ascribed at will to almost any period down to the fifth century B.C. One of the most conspicuous theories derived from this age of Homeric criticism has already been mentioned: according to it, the spirit of Homer and of Ionian civilization as a whole was thoroughly secular; the gods of Homer have ceased to be invariably objects of worship; Homer does not regard the gods with reverence, and in fact did a great deal to dissociate the idea of god from that of worship.

Obviously, if this theory that Homer is a powerful antireligious force is acceptable, the problem that we are investigating is already solved. Ionian philosophers, sympathizing with Homer, may have applied the term "god" to the universe

[4]

or to the primary substance in some non-religious or irreverent sense, and further inquiry into its exact meaning would be like demanding an explanation of every frivolous utterance. It must be admitted that the theory has been recommended by excellent scholars; it is the product of Wilamowitz and Rohde; Eduard Meyer has said that Homer is *"durchaus profan"*; and the theory is plausible. Moreover, its very existence demonstrates the vitality of the attack that Xenophanes and Plato made against Homer; the modern theory is hardly more than a diluted repetition of the old charge that Homer's anthropomorphic gods are fundamentally irreligious.

Curiously enough, the theory that Homer composed a textbook of religion, and spoke as a professional theologian, is equally plausible and has quite as long a history. If the poetry were not so valuable, the fact that these two opinions directly contradict each other would be merely an amusing demonstration of the relativity of human judgment and of the fact that critics live upon different aspects of a poet's genius as parasites live on different branches of a tree. The partisans of this second opinion are quite as respectable as and perhaps more numerous than the partisans of the first; most of the ancient Greeks were among its adherents, and it was as natural for them to believe that Homer was a great religious teacher as it was to represent him as an authority on the arts of war and of eloquence. The famous passage in Herodotus is typical of this opinion: "Homer and Hesiod composed a poetical Theogony for the Hellenes, gave the gods their significant names, assigned to them their proper honors and arts, and indicated the various kinds of them." This is almost wholly true of Hesiod; it is almost wholly false of Homer. Hesiod came near being a professional theologian; Homer did not. The fact that nearly all Greeks accepted, in one way or another, Homer's *obiter dicta* about the gods is indeed a testimony to his influence, but it does not convert him into a theologian. What Homer has to say about the gods is incidental to the necessities of a work of art.

Upon closer examination, it is possible to discern that these apparently contradictory theories rest upon a common basis. They both assume that Homer set out to tell the truth about the gods, and that the poetry can be treated as though it were the work of a professional theologian. Whereupon Xenophanes and Plato, Rohde and Burnet, arrive at the conclusion that Homer is irreverent, secular and anti-religious in tone; and most of antiquity, using the same evidence, arrived at the conclusion that Homer was a great religious teacher. With all due deference, it may be suggested that the original assumption is incorrect, and that only by abandoning it can we remove the screen which its adherents have placed between Homer and us. Undoubtedly Homer can give us instruction, about religion as well as about other things, but we may well at this late date have the courtesy to allow him to teach as an artist teaches. We may be quite certain that he will neither preach nor lecture.

We have now claimed the right to read and to judge the poems of Homer as those of a conscious literary artist. Perhaps it should be noted that the famous theory which regarded the poems as the product of centuries of anonymous poetical activity is at last practically dead. It has spent the last thirty years dying; it was the greatest literary heresy on record; and it kept on living long after the facts which finally overwhelmed it had been discovered. The courage of its supporters was magnificent; and we need not forget that they fought under the banners of *Wissenschaft*, of the sciences of literary and historical criticism, all of which stimulated them, and prolonged their resistance to the facts.[1] Once more we

---

[1] In the nineteenth century, the scholars who maintained that the epics of Homer had been composed by a multitude of anonymous poets, asserted that the results of their criticism were "scientific," i.e. that their analyses were as correct as those made by chemists, because they were founded upon the "science" of literary criticism. Unfortunately for their faith, their analyses of Homer were all different one from another: such differences do not occur

are free to inquire of Homer, and to seek in his poems his personal vision of the world.

Homer's vision of the gods is distinguished, as we should expect, by its inclusiveness and its elasticity. It is not systematic; it does not develop assumptions about the gods to their logical consequences, as it would if Homer were a philosopher or a theologian; it is not mere light-hearted play with the possibilities of polytheistic mythology, as it might be if Homer were irreligious. The world, as Homer sees it, throngs with gods (θεοί, δαίμονες); and the world is throughout effectively governed by divine power. Often this power is represented as being exercised by and belonging to the gods as a collective body; often Zeus alone is represented as wielding this power. If causality were confined to these channels, to the apparently personal and anthropomorphic god or gods, it might be justifiable to describe Homer's religious world as "constructed on the lines of personal theism," or rather let us say polytheism.

Such in fact is the traditional view; Homer is regularly treated as a convinced even though occasionally irreverent believer in personal polytheism. And so he is. But it is of the utmost importance, to the understanding of Homer, to note that this description of his religious beliefs is far from being exhaustive or even roughly adequate, and that his religious world overflows the boundaries of personal polytheism. It would be equally true, although the phrase may sound like a contradiction in terms, to assert that Homer believes in impersonal theism. When we discuss the ideas of a man or of a people whose intellectual heirs we are, we naturally and inevitably apply modern labels to old ways of thinking, and under cover of those labels modern notions steal in and pro-

when chemists analyse the same substance: and finally the irresistible inference was drawn that literary criticism was not a science, but a pseudo-science, and that its results depended for their accuracy not upon a guaranteed method but upon the insight of the particular critic. Meantime, archaeological discoveries shattered all the presuppositions, about the state of Greece in early times, upon which the theory of multiple authorship had originally rested.

duce an appearance of complication and of irrationality in beliefs which were really as simple and perhaps as reasonable as our own. Thus artificial problems are created; and we have an excellent example of such a problem in the difficulties that have been raised about Homer's theism.

Modern thought automatically associates the concept of personality with the concept of theism; Greek thought did not necessarily associate the two concepts. When we use the word "God," we involuntarily regard it as a proper name, as the name of a personal being; and the history of philosophy and of Christianity explains our modern usage. But the Homeric view, and the ordinary Greek view, of the operation of divine power in the universe did not limit it to the effective action of personal beings. Even the word θεός is often used to refer to the action of some anonymous and impersonal divine power; the instances are cited in the Homeric lexicons of Capelle and of Ebeling. Perhaps the clearest proof of the tendency of θεός to be impersonal is the fact that the vocative was never used until a late period. On the other hand, the Greeks could and did pray to the θεοί as a collective body of divine powers, which could be addressed under a single inclusive title precisely as Zeus or other gods, when thought of as personal beings, could be addressed by name.

The fact that Homer did not think of divine power as necessarily exercised by personal beings is amply illustrated by the number and the nature of the terms, in addition to θεός and the names of the apparently personal gods, that he uses to denote the possessors of such power. The principal among these terms are δαίμων and δαίμονες (transcribed as "daimon" and "daimons" to avoid the associations of "demon")[2], μοῖρα and αἶσα ("moira" and "aisa," fate or destiny). Daimon, though often equated with θεός, is often used

[2] The early Christians, who did not dream of denying the existence of the pagan deities, were satisfied to classify the pagan deities as evil divine powers, and called them all δαίμονες (daimons): hence comes the modern use of "demon" to signify an evil divine power.

as the equivalent of "divine power," or "fate" or "fortune"; and Homer's treatment of moira has brought about endless debate, because it raises an artificial problem in its most acute form.

Homer not only feels at liberty to attribute causal power to an unnamed, and therefore more or less impersonal "god" or "daimon"; but he goes much farther, and often represents destiny as possessing the whole sum of divine power. The idea of destiny or of fate is that of an impersonal and unalterable power which governs the succession of events; few altars are raised and few prayers are offered to destiny. Logically, a belief in destiny is incongruous with a belief in personal and omnipotent or quasi-omnipotent gods who listen to prayer, reward their friends and punish their enemies. Homer's belief in an overruling causality is obviously the sort of belief that we call philosophical; it appears to be the result of speculation on the nature of things in general, and particularly, so far as men are concerned, upon the inevitability of death. Hence fate is often synonymous with death. On the other hand, what becomes of the power wielded by a personal Zeus, if fate is really omnipotent?

A plausible solution of this difficulty was proposed by Welcker and adopted by Nägelsbach in his *Homerische Theologie*. It is plausible, because as Gruppe says, "the mightier a god is, the closer his accord with destiny"; but it breaks down completely in just those cases in which Zeus is inclined to have a will of his own, or happens to be unaware of what is really going on. When Zeus wanted to deliver his son Sarpedon from fate, Hera rebuked him, and Zeus "did not disregard her": Zeus, that is, gave up doing what he wanted to do.[3] When Zeus was beguiled by Hera, with the formidable and effective aid of Aphrodite, Love, Desire, and Sleep, the will of the great god was far from being identical with fate.[4] Agamemnon endeavors to excuse his quarrel with

[3] *Iliad*, XVI, 431 *ff.*   [4] *ibid.*, XIV, 153 *ff.*

Achilles on the ground that even Zeus, on another occasion, was deceived by Hera and blinded by Ate (Ruinous Folly), so that Zeus, contrary to his own desire, was driven to glorify Eurystheus.[5] Did Homer seriously intend to equate with destiny the will of this god Zeus, who is so often the plaything of ignorance and of blind passion?

The real solution does not lie in the identification of the will of a personal god with destiny, but in quite another direction. The difficulty disappears, and the inconsistency in the relations between personal gods and destiny is resolved, the moment we remind ourselves that Homer may have used, and did use, the word "Zeus" in several different senses. The suggestion may at first seem faintly reprehensible. Our involuntary tendency is to exclaim, with Mr. Farnell, that "when Homer speaks of Zeus he meant Zeus."[6] And it is perfectly true that we habitually think of a proper noun as surrendering its meaning *en bloc*: Zeus would mean Zeus as Smith means Smith. However, mental habits are not secure guides. The suggestion that in dealing with Homer we must ask which Zeus he means, just as we should now ask which Smith was meant, originally comes from Plutarch, who said that Homer often meant destiny or fortune when he used the word "Zeus" (*De Aud. Poet.*, 23E).

There is a whole family of gods named Zeus in the pages of Homer, just as there is a whole family of gods named Zeus in the history of Greek cult: the fact that under a single name there lie different characters and meanings was familiar not only to Plutarch but to all thoughtful Greeks. No Greek felt the slightest difficulty in distinguishing the savage Zeus who was worshipped in Arcadia and who demanded human sacrifice, from the kindly Zeus who protected the stranger-guest (Zeus Xenios); and Homer relied upon epithet or context to clarify his references to Zeus, precisely as later Greeks would pray to Zeus Ktesios (of Acquisition) to save and increase

[5] *Iliad*, XIX, 91 ff.   [6] *Cults of the Greek States*, I, 79.

their wealth or to Zeus Herkeios (of the House-Altar) to sanction the duties of child to parent and parent to child. The personal and anthropomorphic Zeus who laments the death of Sarpedon is vastly different from the impersonal or depersonalized Zeus whose will is identical with destiny. The difference in meaning is directly caused by the intention of the poet. In one case Homer refers to the very human god who had loved the heroine Laodameia, mother of Sarpedon, and the context is that of kinship, of affection, and of human passion; in the other case, Homer is thinking of the chain of events, and of the great divine impersonal power which seems to have forged the chain, and which is raised far above human suffering. The one Zeus is subordinate to destiny; the other Zeus is destiny. The two divine powers bear the same name, but have little else in common.

The conclusion at once emerges that Homer's conception of divinity is far more elastic and embracing than it would be if his mind operated only within the limits set by an anthropomorphic personal polytheism. It is not a systematic conception, it is full of degrees and shades of meaning; but in general it may be said that while anthropomorphic gods naturally and inevitably are conspicuous causal agents in the story told by Homer, nevertheless Homer does not regard these human characteristics as an indispensable attribute of divinity. The depersonalized Zeus who is almost identical with destiny, and destiny itself, are preeminently divine, and they are also preeminently causal: they are the divine source of all events, they are the power that rules the world.

Homer in fact speaks as though there were a reservoir of divine power in the world, which may manifest itself impersonally, and is then called moira or aisa or the will of Zeus, "god" or "the gods" or daimon; or else it may manifest itself through named deities who are in varying degrees endowed with human characteristics. Homer's picture of divinity is rich and varied: one is tempted to think that it has perhaps no solid nucleus and no single element that is common to all these manifestations. But the solid nucleus and the common element exist; the very substance and the one elementary principle of divinity is power.

The Greeks in general remained true to the Homeric intuition of divinity. Some five hundred years after Homer's time, Menander remarked that "that which possesses power is now worshipped as a god"—

$$\tau\grave{o} \ \kappa\rho\alpha\tau o\hat{v}\nu \ \gamma\grave{\alpha}\rho \ \nu\hat{v}\nu \ \nu o\mu\acute{\iota}\zeta\epsilon\tau\alpha\iota \ \theta\epsilon\acute{o}s.^{[7]}$$

The remark, being made about Shamelessness, is tinged with irony, but is none the less accurate. If we accept this idea of divinity as a working hypothesis and test it, we shall find abundant confirmation.

It is unnecessary to enumerate all the natural powers that Homer divinizes. Okeanos (the divine river that surrounds the world) is called the "source of being" ($\gamma\acute{\epsilon}\nu\epsilon\sigma\iota s$) of all gods; Tethys, his wife and the mother of all gods, is the divine "nurse"; and among their offspring are the Sun (Helios), Night, Dawn (Eos), and the Seasons (Horai), Amphitrite the sea "deep-voiced who feeds countless flocks," the river gods, the nymphs, the gods of the winds. Death and Sleep are great natural powers of another sort, and they are divinized as Thanatos and Hypnos. We have seen that Zeus, stripped of human qualities, may become divine Destiny; Homer did not hesitate to make him undergo another metamorphosis in the phrase "The cry of the two hosts went up through the higher air, to the splendor of Zeus," where Zeus has become the Sky. So Ares is transformed in the phrase "praying for escape from death and the tumult of Ares," where Ares is Battle; and Hephaistos becomes Fire in the phrase "they spitted the vitals and held them over Hephaistos."[8] The name means the powerful element, and the element is divine.

A magnificent example of the divinization of a natural power is found in Book XXI of the *Iliad*. It is the moment

---

[7] Kock, *Comicorum atticorum fragmenta*, 261.
[8] *Iliad*, XIII, 837; II, 401; II, 426.

when the final conflict between Achilles and Hector is imminent, and Homer in a scene of the wildest grandeur narrates the flight of Achilles before the flood of the river Xanthos, and the rescue of Achilles by the divine Fire (Hephaistos) which conquers the divine River. The world and the powers within it come alive before our eyes; or perhaps it would be nearer the truth to say that the genius of Homer sharpens our vision, and for once we see the living and divine universe which is strange to our minds and which was familiar to the Greeks.

Homer treats as divinities another set of forces that operate in human life. Such are the gods Fear (Deimos), Terror (Phobos), the goddess War (Enyo), Strife (Eris), Ruinous Folly (Ate), Prayers (Litai), the Graces (Charites), Rumor (Ossa), and Justice (Themis). Nothing could better illustrate the uneasiness of the modern mind in the presence of a belief that it no longer understands than the fact that these gods are habitually called personifications. To personify means to attribute a personal nature to an abstraction. From what point of view is Phobos an abstraction? It would be too bad to introduce the old quarrel of the schoolmen, and to talk about considering the form of terror apart from the matter of terror. Homer and the Greeks made Terror into a god because it was a real power. On the other hand, Mr. Farnell says that the projection of a strong mental emotion into the unseen world without, and its identification with "some vague 'numen' of divine causative power" is a mark not of "later reflective thought, but of a primitive habit of mind."[9]

Let us be modest, and regard with suspicion all statements that delicately flatter us by pointing out a contrast between our modern reflective thought and primitive habits of mind. In this particular case, it may or may not be primitive to ascribe divinity to power; but once that step is taken, there

---

[9] *op. cit.*, V, 444.

is nothing especially primitive about ascribing a kind of real existence and activity to terror or to justice. Bréal, in his treatment of such "abstractions," wisely remarks that "even at the present day—so great is the continuity of things—those who discuss matter, force, substance, perpetuate more or less this ancient condition of mind."[10] At any rate, we must remember that these gods were not felt by the Greeks to have been manufactured or invented, as the term "personification" implies; they were discovered and recognized, precisely as a modern scientist discovers and recognizes the effects of something that he calls "electricity."

Other scholars, opposing Mr. Farnell's view, have maintained that such gods as Terror and Justice cannot belong to an early period, because "the primitive language does not deal with philosophic or abstract terms, and the physical and concrete precede the immaterial and abstract." We are so thoroughly accustomed to the complacent evolutionary scheme which arranges the history of thought, of religion, of language, and of almost every human activity as a progress from the lower to the higher, from the primitive to the civilized, from the worse to the better, that we are inclined to accept without scrutiny any statement that shows how much higher, better and more civilized we are than any previous generation. Change is certain; possibilities of progress have been accumulated by constant toil and by sporadic genius through many thousands of years; but so far we have succeeded in realizing and exploiting, for the most part, only our undoubted capacity for making tools. *Homo faber* is far ahead of *homo sapiens;* and for this reason the assumption of automatic progress is absurd. The notion that Homer is likely to be less "sophisticated" or more "primitive" than Aristotle, simply because one preceded the other in time, is a form of Narcissism. The Greek language, in Homer's day, was centuries removed from a primitive condition; and it is not true that

[10] *Semantics* (Eng. tr., London, 1900), 246.

language, as a rule, moves from the concrete to the abstract. It also moves, and at the same time, in the other direction; names of actions and states have passed and still pass into the names of concrete objects. The same process by which a Greek of Homer's time recognized a divinity in Justice was confidently followed by the later Greeks who said that "the fact of success" was a "god," and that the thrill of meeting a friend was a "god."[11] These gods are not at all abstractions. But of course they may appear abstract to one who is not in sympathy with them, exactly as the Aristotelian definition of God as "thought thinking itself" may seem abstract to one who does not agree with Aristotle, but meant to Aristotle the highest and most perfect reality.

So far then the general impression that Homer's gods are "robust and sharply defined personalities, conceived in the glorified image of man," turns out to be erroneous; it applies only to a small number of those gods. The evidence shows that it is the possession of power, and not of human characteristics, that generates the Homeric god. Moreover, Homer himself conceives his anthropomorphic gods as admitting their inferiority to certain rival gods who have nothing human about them. The Greeks had a custom of taking an oath upon every possible public or private occasion. The oath (ὄρκος) was held to be a restraint (ἕρκος) upon liberty; and the Greeks, aware (as Glotz remarks in his excellent essay upon the oath)[12] that "the habit of swearing soon leads to forswearing," always chose gods as witnesses, on the ground that the superior power of the gods ensured the due punishment of the human perjurer. "The god Oath has a nameless son, who has no hands or feet, but who never ceases his violent pursuit till he has seized and utterly destroyed all who belong to the family of the perjured man." This belief in the vengeance of the gods who had been invoked as witnesses re-

[11] cf. the valuable discussion in Gilbert Murray's *Five Stages of Greek Religion*, 26 ff.
[12] *Etudes sur l'antiquité grecque*, 99 ff.

mained living throughout Greek history. The question at once arises, what gods will Homer choose as witnesses to an oath taken by one of his human gods? Here we have a privileged case, because the answer must reveal the names of gods whom Homer believed to be more powerful than those who swear. These mightier gods are Sky (Ouranos), Earth (Gaia), and the falling Water of Styx: "the greatest oath and the most terrible to the blessed gods," as Hera says (*Iliad*, XV, 36*ff*.). The highest powers are therefore those which represent the divine universe; and if to these three we add Destiny, and the non-human Zeus who is equivalent to Destiny, and the inclusive plural "gods" when used to refer to the sum of divine power, we have a complete list of the highest divine powers that Homer recognizes. None of these highest powers is really anthropomorphic. And yet the tradition about Homer's gods is stubborn; it refuses to be lightly dismissed, and it reminds us that despite the evidence our dominant impression of Homer's gods is that of their human, all-too-human nature and conduct. Fortunately the explanation of this puzzle lies at hand.

In obedience to the principle that power is divine, the Greeks of every period attributed a portion of divinity to men whose power was above the normal human level. Such men were called heroes, a name which in Greek is the regular technical designation of a status which is intermediate between that of an ordinary man and that of a god. The bestowal of this status was usually limited to conspicuous individuals and to groups of warriors who had fallen in battle; but in the special case of the Mycenaean Greeks, their descendants, that is to say all Greeks of historic times, were so filled with awe at the tradition of Mycenaean glory and power that they conferred heroic status upon the whole mass of their ancestors, and called their age the Heroic Age. Homer was attempting, with deliberate and fully conscious archaism, to portray a dramatic action of the Heroic Age which preceded his own; and he was forced to give the anthropomorphic gods a central place in the action by the political, social and religious tradition concerning the heroes.[13]

To the Greek mind, the most natural method of expressing the belief that a hero is partly divine was the method of affiliation. In historic times, it was obviously difficult to ascribe direct divine parentage to a man whose life and whose actual human parents were well known, and the Greeks were as a rule content to bestow partly divine status upon a hero without attempting to relate him to a god. But in the case of the Mycenaean Greeks, who were known only by tradition and by the visible relics of their power, no such obstacle existed; and their descendants, giving free rein to their belief and to their fancy, related every important hero of that age to a god. Critics who no longer share or even sympathize with that ancient faith have found it easy to deride the divine "machinery" in Homer. If they would put themselves in Homer's place, and by some magic endow themselves with his powerful and accurate imagination, they would discover that they would be compelled to repeat in all its essentials Homer's own picture of the anthropomorphic gods, and that they had mistaken for "easy scepticism" and for a "mocking, half-licentious, Boccaccio-like spirit" what was in reality the combination of poetic genius with profound religious faith.

Homer's faith was not our faith, but that is no excuse for not attempting to understand it. The gods to him represented power. Some of these gods, the greatest among them, were thoroughly unhuman powers; even Zeus, when Zeus means Destiny, is unhuman. Other gods, in accordance with universal Greek tradition, were the parents, by union with a mortal, of the heroes; and the greatest heroes were singled out to become the children, at one or more removes, of the greatest available gods. But only one of the greatest and

---

[13] cf. on this whole subject the brilliant and sound Chapter xviii, by J. B. Bury, in the *Cambridge Ancient History*, Vol. II; on hero cult, the *Greek Hero Cults* of Farnell and the *Culte des héros* of Foucart; and an article on Homer and hero cult by the author, in *Transactions of the American Philological Association*, Vol. LX (1929).

more or less unhuman gods had a name which was sufficiently vague to render him available; a hero could not be the son of Moira or of Ouranos, but he could be the son of Zeus. Hence a vast burden of paternity was imposed upon Zeus, and after him upon those lesser gods whose names were also vague, unmeaning, and personal. It is easy to forget that a personal name such as Zeus or Athene or Aphrodite does not of itself define the power that is attributed to its possessor; even the name of a river-god is far more eligible as that of an ancestor than the name of the goddess Justice. Thus it came about that by the time of Homer many gods were fulfilling a double function; they were not only the representatives by tradition of certain special powers which were the very substance of their divinity, but they were also heads of families. These families became more human and less divine with each passing generation; and Homer, together with every Greek who shared the traditional faith, was forced to imagine the gods who were heads of families as possessed of all human characteristics except those which are incompatible with the permanent possession of power. The picture that Homer gives of these gods is the picture of a true believer.

Join the possession of superhuman power to human traits, take seriously the belief in heroes, and the result is the anthropomorphic gods in Homer. They are exempt from death, since power does not die; they are endowed with superhuman knowledge, since knowledge is one form of power, and is an attribute of Psyche, i.e. of Life and Soul; the rest of their character and conduct is a precise and formidably true portrayal of the effect that the possession of such power would have upon immortal men and women. Much of the story resembles comedy, or even farce; but that is inevitable, since the greatest human penalty, the penalty of death, is missing, except in so far as these gods are touched by sorrow at the death of their heroic descendants. The other source of tragedy, second to death, is the fact of the unalterable past into which human acts recede; and it is true that these gods make mistakes and commit sins, but the heaviness of their errors is cancelled by the fact that unlike men they have all time before them.

The anthropomorphism of these gods is essentially the price that Greek religion paid for hero worship and the consequent attempt to relate certain gods to men. The only difference between the picture of them given by Homer, and that which was in the mind of an ordinary Greek, is the difference due to Homer's artistic genius, which enabled him to realize all the implications of the faith that he shared with his fellows. We must admit that such a picture, when once adequately thought out, was bound to present many features which, though they left the orthodox multitudes unstirred except by the charm of the narrative, would now and then shock some stray heretical reformer. That is the sole concession that we ought to make to the critics of Homer's "wicked" gods and "irreligious" tone. When Homer is judged as an artist, within the limitations imposed by his time, he cannot be blamed for failing to anticipate and to comply with the new and different religious requirements of Xenophanes and of Plato.

The anthropomorphic gods, though they play a great part in the poems, are merely one element in Homer's intuition of divinity. They represent Homer's conviction that certain divine powers are akin to, although remote from, ordinary mankind; and we have already seen that in several cases, when Homer is thinking of the power alone, its cloak of humanity completely disappears and the naked power is left. Zeus easily, "as befits a god," becomes destiny; Hephaistos loses his limp and becomes divine Fire. It has been said that such uses of the word "god" are non-religious, on the ground that "in its religious sense the word 'god' always means first and foremost an object of worship, but already in Homer that has ceased to be its only signification." Hesiod's *Theogony* is said to be the best evidence of this change in meaning: "it is clear that many of the gods mentioned there were never worshipped by any one, and some of them are mere personifications of natural phenomena, or even of human passions."[14] The question here raised is of vital importance to the understanding of Greek thought. What is the relation between the three ideas—god, worship, and power?

So far as Homer and Greek religious tradition are concerned, it is impossible to dissociate the idea of god and of divinity from the idea of power. Every god is thought of as a power; every power that rises above the ordinary human level is thought of as a god, or at least as partly divine. We have already analysed the "mere personifications" of natural phenomena and of human passions, and we have seen that Homer regards them as powers and as divine. Does Homer worship all the divine powers that he recognizes? The question may be answered by another question: does worship consist in the payment of outward observances, in audible prayer, in kneeling, in the offer of sacrifice? Such acts are surely no more than the token of a mental attitude; the reality of worship lies in the recognition, by man, of powers superior to his own; it is not true that such recognition always leads to some outward observance; it is not true, for that matter, that the outward observance is an infallible guarantee of genuine inner worship. As for Homer, no one knows what altars he raised or what sacrifices he made; his poems are his only testimony; but their credibility is confirmed by all the known facts of Greek outer cult. The cult of the divine Winds (Anemoi) was frequent, and Boreas was a land-owning citizen of Thurii; the Sun was regularly worshipped; the cult of Earth was not rare; Rivers were everywhere worshipped, and along with them the Nymphs of springs, trees, and mountains. In the other category, the Muses, the Graces, the Fates, the goddesses of the Curse (Erinyes), Victory, Reverence, Pity, Laughter, and Terror were known to all Greeks, and the cult of most of them was common. Therefore we conclude that these and similar gods are not non-religious, either in the

---

[14] J. Burnet, *Early Greek Philosophy*[3], 14.

pages of Homer or anywhere else. Why then do excellent modern scholars attempt to deny these facts?

The answer is simple and illuminating. These scholars dread that if the facts are admitted, they may fall into the "error of deriving science from mythology," and that the "god" of the Ionian philosophers may lose the "complete independence of religious tradition" that they claim for it. We have already seen that the gods of Homer are not independent of religious tradition; we shall soon see that the philosophers and men of science of Ionia were not miraculously liberated from religious tradition. Speculative thought is not, like Rousseau's imaginary man, born free. It is not even the exclusive property of philosophers and men of science; poets have ideas, though they are not likely to present their thought in systematic form, and though we always do some degree of injustice to a poet when we report his thought. In this connection, it should be remembered that philosophers, like the frog in the fable, have invariably ruined their own ideas when they have blown them up into a system.

The multiplicity of divine powers that Homer recognizes is startling enough; the differences between the human and the non-human group are disconcerting to a modern; even the names of his gods are not stable, but have now one and now another meaning. Nevertheless, in some ways these divine powers are all alike. First, they are all manifestations of power over the universe, or some part of it, and therefore over man. Second, they are all immortal. Third, one divinity, Okeanos, is named the Source of Being ($\gamma \acute{\epsilon} \nu \epsilon \sigma \iota s$), from whom all other gods (including Sky and Earth) descend, and men as well; though immortal, all other gods have come into being, and are a part of the history of the universe. The essential characteristics of the Homeric god are therefore the possession of power, of life, and of a place in cosmic history. Anthropomorphism is not an indispensable adjunct; moral perfection is not an indispensable adjunct. Power is not necessarily moral; on the contrary, from man's point of view, many

powers are evil, and Homer is rarely more eloquent than
when he ridicules Ares, who when wounded "bellowed loud
as nine thousand warriors, or ten thousand, cry in battle," and
who asked Zeus, in a speech of marvellous irony, whether
Zeus had no indignation at beholding these violent deeds.[15]
Not Xenophanes, not Plato, was a more severe critic than
Homer of the anthropomorphic gods when they did what was
evil in the sight of man; the difference between Homer and
the philosophers is not at all that he is less morally sensitive,
but that he still believes in the reality of these gods. It is
Homer, not Cleanthes, who first suggests that the gods may
evade their causative responsibility for evil by attributing
evil to man's own follies; but neither Homer nor any philosopher has yet explained how the gods can evade responsibility
without ceasing to be causes. The whole speech of Zeus, in
Book I of the *Odyssey*, should be consulted, and with it we
should take into account the numerous passages in which
Homer identifies divine Destiny with "that which ought to
be," and so asserts the ultimate goodness of the universe. Nor
is Homer's moral tone a question of stray passages; James
Adam, in his valuable treatise *The Religious Teachers of
Greece*, has rightly pointed out that the "action of the *Iliad*
and *Odyssey*, regarded as a whole, fulfils the law that 'the
doer must suffer'." And yet critics have ventured to de-
nounce as "mocking scepticism" the very scenes in which
Homer upholds the moral law, even at the expense of his
gods. Homer, now in the Elysian fields, is perhaps not sur-
prised at being misunderstood.

Before leaving Homer, let us recur to the god Okeanos.
Homer does not discuss this belief in a non-anthropomorphic
god as the source of the universe; he merely takes it for
granted, and thereby doubles the weight of his testimony. The
idea was already current that the universe, and all other gods,
sprang from a divine source; and the importance of this idea
in subsequent Greek thought can hardly be exaggerated.

[15] *Iliad*, V, 864 *ff*. Zeus, in reply, called Ares " ἀλλοπρόσαλλος " (fickle, going
from one to another), and told him not to whine.

CHAPTER III

HESIOD

THE Hesiodic *Theogony* is the work of a poet who is far less the artist and far more the professional theologian than Homer. Its author not only named a multitude of the gods whose power directly affects human life, Memory, Doom, Blame, Woe, Indignation, Deceit, Friendship, Old Age, Forgetfulness (Lethe), Toil, and many others, but also added a long list of gods who belong to the natural history of the universe, such as Chaos the yawning gulf which was the source of being, Earth, Love, Erebos, Night, Aither,[1] Day, Sky, Sea, Nile, Alpheios, and the Moon. The poet could not have made more clear his belief that the universe is essentially a divine power. Except in details, such as the substitution of Chaos for Okeanos, and the unexplained appearance of Love, Hesiod makes the divine non-anthropomorphic powers appear successively in much the same order that Homer might have followed if he had been a theologian. With Hesiod as with Homer, every power is a god, and one among these powers is the source of all others.

On the surface, Hesiod's conception of divinity closely resembles the less sharply defined notions of Homer. Zeller, the greatest of all historians of Greek philosophy, gives Hesiod a place in his work, with the remark that "Though it would be a mistake to place the mythic cosmologists . . . in the number of the philosophers, . . . yet we ought not, on the other hand, to underrate the importance of these early attempts, for they were at least useful in calling attention to

[1] I have transliterated the Greek αἰθήρ (the gleaming upper air) to avoid the associations of the English derivative.

the questions which science had first to consider, and in accustoming thought to combine particular phenomena under general points of view; and thus a good deal was done towards a beginning of science." Zeller goes on to speak of Hesiod's "childlike curiosity," and suggests that the poet was guided, in dealing with the problem of the primitive condition of the world and its ulterior development, by the intuitions of his imagination and not by intelligent reflection. Since Zeller's time, scholars have been inclined to attach more weight to Hesiod's contribution to Greek thought; Burnet says that "the rudiments of what grew into Ionic science and history are to be found in his poems."[2] Robin speaks of Hesiod's effort to "perceive a relation of subordination between realities, to discover a common basis of things that will serve as the foundation of all future change"; and asserts that "rational thought will only continue this effort of the mythical theogony and cosmogony; in transforming this effort by a change of orientation, it will produce the illusion of an entirely new and almost spontaneous creation, whereas in reality it will only develop a previously existing germ."[3] Mazon, in the introduction to his excellent edition of Hesiod, suggests that behind the myth of the mutilation of Ouranos, which puts an end to his disordered fertility, and the myth of the birth of Aphrodite, there lies the idea of the fixity of species; "perhaps the Platonic theory of Ideas is only a refined translation of the very simple sentiment that animated the unknown inventor of this myth." How great is the real difference between the thought of Hesiod and the thought of Homer?

In mere native power of mind and art, Homer is vastly superior to Hesiod; the difference between the ideas of the two poets concerning the gods is due, in considerable measure, to this difference in mental equipment. Hesiod is confused where Homer is clear and sparkling. Even in the invocation of the Muses, at the opening of the *Theogony*, it is not quite

[2] *Early Greek Philosophy*[3], 6.
[3] *La pensée grecque*, 33.

clear what the Muses mean when they say to Hesiod, while he was shepherding his lambs under holy Helicon, "O shepherds who dwell in the fields, wretched things of shame, mere bellies, we know how to recount many inventions which are like unto the truth, and when we will, we know how to utter what is unerring." Mazon takes the passage to mean that the rude shepherds believe poetry to be mere *"fiction et jeu,"* whereas Hesiod is commissioned to prove that poetry is also truth. But Hesiod may have intended the allusion to fictitious poetry as a criticism of Homer or of earlier epic in general; and even when due allowance is made for the possibilities of interpolation, the structure of Hesiod's thought is often cloudy.

In still greater measure, the difference between the religious ideas of the two poets is due to the complete divergence of their intentions. Hesiod concludes his invocation of the Muses with these remarkable lines:

"Hail, children of Zeus! Grant lovely song, and celebrate the holy race of immortals who are for ever, those that were born of Earth and of starry Sky and of dark Night, and those that salt Sea reared. Tell how at the first gods and Earth came to be, and Rivers, and boundless Sea with its rushing swell, and the gleaming Stars, and wide Sky above, and the gods who were born of these gods and are the givers of good things; tell how these latter gods divided their wealth and how they shared their honors, and how at the first they took Olympus of the many ravines. Relate to me this story, O Muses who dwell on Olympus, from the beginning, and tell me which of them first came to be." Obviously the opinion of Robin is correct; here we have rational thought devoting itself to the beginnings of the universe and its subsequent history, and to the origin and subsequent history of the gods. The two tasks are still regarded as one; Hesiod still believes in and worships the "anthropomorphic" gods, no less than he believes in the gods who are explicitly powers of nature. Nevertheless, this pious theologian has begun the process which soon rendered belief in the anthropomorphic gods impossible to a few of the more thoughtful Greeks.

For one thing, Hesiod arranges the gods in two groups. The first group, in point of time, is the immortal powers of the universe; the second group consists of the Olympian gods, whose supreme master is Zeus. The Olympians, through the victory of Zeus and his generosity, have inherited the powers which belonged to their predecessors, and are represented as "the givers of good things" (δωτῆρες ἑάων). The old ambiguities which we found in Homer still persist; the name of an Olympian god, apparently personal, may at any moment occur in a transparent allegory, as in the story of the marriage of Zeus to Thought (Metis), and of his marriage to Justice, who bore the Seasons and Order and Peace and the Fates. And yet Hesiod has done what Homer did not do; he has drawn a line of division between these two groups of gods, and has concentrated our attention by the story he tells upon the events that separate them.

According to Hesiod, there are five generations of gods. Chaos is the primogenitor; Earth, Love, Erebos, and Night are the second generation; the most important members of the third generation are Sky, Sea, Okeanos, Rhea, Justice, Memory, the Titans (of whom Kronos is one), the Cyclopes, the Giants, the Erinyes, Aphrodite, Aither, Day, the Destinies, Strife, and Forgetfulness (Lethe); among the members of the fourth generation are the Rivers, the Nymphs, Sun, Moon, Dawn, Styx, Leto, Hecate, Hestia, Demeter, Hera, Hades, Poseidon, Zeus, Atlas, and Prometheus; and in the fifth are Peace, the Graces, Persephone, the Muses, Apollo, Artemis, Ares, Athene, Hephaistos, Hermes, and Dionysus.

Three decisive events lead up to the victory of Zeus. First, the fertility of Sky is terminated, at the advice of Earth, by Kronos (vv. 147-210), and the Titans under Kronos reign; second, Kronos is beguiled by Rhea, Earth, and Sky into permitting the birth of Zeus and five other gods, who at the advice of Earth make war from Olympus against the Titans and are finally successful; third, the supremacy of Zeus is recognized by all the gods, the Titans are banished, and the present age of the world begins, in which Zeus and his subordinates are especially the "givers of good things."

In this last age, Earth, Sky, and all the other divine powers of the universe still exist; disorder has ceased; and Zeus, along with a group of his brothers and sisters and children, has been rendered far more historical and personal than were the gods of Homer. The proper names of these gods, which in Homer were often mere transparent covers for other meanings, have been stuffed full of events by the narrative of Hesiod; and while this narrative has strong allegorical tendencies, and Hesiod ventures on one occasion to anthropomorphize even the Sky, the net result is a marked contrast between the oldest and the youngest gods, between the divine powers of nature and the highly personal gods like Zeus, who now have a fairly complete history.

The line of demarcation thus drawn between the two kinds of gods was obviously dangerous, and was ultimately fatal, to the anthropomorphic group. It is not that the danger was obvious to Hesiod; both kinds were to him still sacred ($\iota\epsilon\rho\acute{o}\nu$) and held in reverence ($\alpha\grave{\iota}\delta o\widehat{\iota}o\nu$). It is probable that Hesiod's zeal led him to enumerate some gods in each group who may never have received outer cult from any Greek; but since the few gods who may not have received outer cult are perfectly analogous to many others who did receive such cult, we are not entitled to stigmatize any of them as "nonreligious." Hesiod was unable to foresee that his partial separation of the anthropomorphic gods from the gods who were powers of nature would in the long run prove ruinous to the anthropomorphic gods.

The anthropomorphic gods were now in the perilous position of being utterly dependent upon the faith of their worshippers; their lives hung by this thread; the moment any one ceased to believe in their real existence, that moment they ceased, for him, to exist. Contrast their position with that of the immortal powers of the universe, who will continue to exist whether any human being believes in them or not. To tell the history of a god is to offer at least a partial explanation of that god; and Hesiod, by offering his explanation, which, although naïve, gives him a right to be classified among those who try to philosophize, had derived the anthropomorphic gods from the far less anthropomorphic immortal powers of the universe. But it is clear enough to us that the anthropomorphic gods could not permanently endure either this or any other explanation.

Explanation is the two-edged sword of philosophy. When it is applied to a reality, it cuts always deeper but never destroys the reality; when it is applied to unrealities, they slowly and reluctantly vanish. Hesiod had a passion for explanations. When he wanted to give a humorous explanation of the evil in the world, he told the story of Pandora; the trouble with mankind is woman, and the reason why woman exists is the anger of Zeus at being cheated by Prometheus. When he wanted a more serious explanation, he told of man's progressive degeneration during the ages. He explained the order of the universe by ascribing it to the divine power of an apparently personal being named Zeus, and he explained Zeus as the grandson of Sky and Earth. Thus Hesiod made the apparently personal gods into a kind of equivalent to or translation from the divine powers of the universe. The majority of Greeks naturally remained content with this and similar stories, and accepted the narration without ever troubling themselves to think of its meaning; but a considerable minority shared Hesiod's love of history and of explanations, and thereby contributed to the disappearance of the anthropomorphic gods.

Another method of explanation, much practised by Hesiod, is the method of allegory. If we may, for our purpose, define allegory as the description of one thing in terms of another which is supposed to be similar, we see at once that allegory does not necessarily explain; it is a literary device which may

[28]

be used on different levels and exploited for various ends. In the simpler forms of metaphor and simile, it may be a most effective stimulus to understanding; but allegories grow colder as they are expanded. Saintsbury called allegories an "endemic disease"; painful as they may be, they are not so bad as the parallel disease of religious and philosophical apologetic, which insists on discovering allegory where none was intended by the author, and which fastened with peculiar virulence upon Homer and Hesiod. However, there is plenty of genuine allegory in Hesiod. To give a god a significant name is already a mild form of allegory: it suggests that the god is equal to some intelligible concept multiplied by divinity, and we have seen that Hesiod is fond of such allegories. He explains Aphrodite as the goddess born from the foam ($\dot{α}φρός$) of the flesh of Ouranos, and the Titans as those who "strained ($τιταίνοντας$) and did presumptuously a fearful deed." Strength (Kratos) and Force (Bia) "have no house apart from Zeus, nor any dwelling nor path except that wherein god leads them." The myth of Pandora contains an allegorical description of woman as a divinely manufactured evil, "not to be withstood by men"; Sleep "roams peacefully over the earth," but Death has a heart of iron; and at least three of the marriages of Zeus are allegories. The first marriage is a little strange; Zeus swallows Metis (Intelligence), and Athene, "equal to her father in strength and in wise understanding," is promptly born from the head of Zeus. The second marriage is with Justice; the children are the Seasons, Order, Law, Peace, and the Fates. The third marriage, with Memory, brings forth the Muses. All these allegories and more are to be found in the *Theogony*. In the *Works and Days* Hesiod gives us the famous allegory of the two Strifes, one of whom is Virtuous Emulation and the other the evil spirit of Quarrel; he adds the obscure allegory of Hope and the jar of evils to the myth of Pandora; and in his description of the Iron Age, he prophesies that Conscience (Aidos) and Righteous Indignation (Nemesis), "with their sweet forms

[29]

wrapped in white robes, will go from the wide-pathed earth and forsake mankind to join the company of the deathless gods."

These are all conscious allegories, and most of them were invented to explain some god or his attributes. Each new allegory about Zeus explains Zeus a little more thoroughly and contributes a new element to our conception of Zeus; each allegory, though it contains some anthropomorphic terms, such as marriage or the statement that one god "attends" another or "swallows" another, also contains terms which are non-anthropomorphic, such as Force, Peace, the Seasons and Intelligence. If Hesiod, and Greek tradition, had been able to limit the offspring of Zeus to gods with personal names, such as Apollo, Artemis, or Persephone, the real being of Zeus would in so far have remained a mystery; but every time that Zeus was represented as having such children as Peace, or such wives as Intelligence or Memory, the mystery of Zeus was in so far diminished, and his real being became proportionately accessible to human intelligence. The net result of Hesiod's use of allegory was the partial reduction of Zeus, the apparently personal god, into a list of divine attributes devoid of personality. When this is combined with the Zeus who results from Hesiod's history, the total is a supreme god, descended from the divine source of the universe, and largely definable as himself the divine source of order in the universe and of justice and intelligence and virtue among men. The mantle of anthropomorphism about the Zeus of Hesiod has worn very thin, and the name "Zeus" has become, for intellectual and religious purposes, a convenient symbol which encloses a given quantity and quality of divine power, and which like the symbols of algebra lacks personality and may be easily transferred to any point in a series or from side to side of an equation.

As for the lesser gods, they have in varying degrees undergone the same process; we need here only to recall that some of them are realities, whose continued existence is quite independent of the faith of any worshipper.

Three features of the ideas now current about the gods and the universe deserve especial emphasis. It is now and henceforth, until the time of Pythagoras, taken for granted that some single natural reality is the divine origin of all things, including the subsequent gods. Second, there is a growing interest in the name and nature of this divine origin; this interest is proved by the fact that Hesiod definitely departs from the choice of Homer, and by the fact that many other theogonies were being composed during this period, some of which differed both from Homer and from Hesiod in their choice of the divine origin. Third, the idea is already current that the nature and the power of a god or of a human being can be explained by and is the result of the substance from which he springs. This last idea is of course related to the ordinary idea of descent from one generation to another, according to which the Greeks explained (for example) the partial divinity and power of the heroes by attributing one divine ancestor to each hero; but it represents an important advance in speculative thought. Hesiod deals with two stages of this idea; in the first, one divine power, without sexual union, produces another. Erebos and Night are thus produced from Chaos; in the same way, Earth produces Sky, and Night most of her offspring. In the second stage, the notion of substance becomes still more prominent. Pandora is manufactured out of earth, clothes, and jewelry; and Aphrodite, goddess of love, springs directly from the fertile substance of a portion of Sky.

This notion of an active substance, which without the intervention of any other agent can produce something resembling itself, was of course destined to have the most profound influence upon Greek thought. Thales and his followers availed themselves of it to explain the universe; and, in particular, it was employed by Greek theologians and philosophers in their doctrines concerning human life and the human soul. By the seventh century B.C., Dionysiac and Orphic theologians had begun to familiarize Greeks with the belief that mankind had sprung from the ashes of the Titans, who had eaten the god Zagreus. The wickedness in man was therefore due to the wickedness of the Titans, and the divine element in man was the transmitted substance of Zagreus. The normal Greek belief held that the soul and life (ψυχή) of man was a portion of divine Air or Fire.

CHAPTER IV

TRANSITION

SO FAR as the available evidence goes, Homer's ideas concerning the gods and the history of the universe, together with Hesiod's modifications of them, constituted the general stock of Greek doctrine on these subjects during the eighth and seventh centuries B.C. The only addition that was made to this stock was the new and exciting doctrine of the mystery religions; apart from that, the only important changes that occurred consist in the accentuation of tendencies already present in the thought of Hesiod.

Homer and Hesiod had left mankind far removed from the gods who were their ancestors; and had promised a happy immortality after death to only a few of the most favored heroes. Hesiod, observing the hints of Homer about the degeneracy of the present generation of men, has expanded them into his eloquent portrayal of the Iron Age; he in his turn hints that the only real hope of mankind lies in the extinction of this race and the recommencement of the cycle of change, a suggestion which became a dogma in many Greek philosophies.[1] It is no wonder that the mystery religions, which guaranteed a happy immortality to all their adherents, swept Greece. The conditions upon which this grant was made vary from the elaborate ritual at Eleusis, little encumbered by dogma or by interference with the ordinary life of the initiated, to the Orphic system, which combined ritual with an elaborate theology and an ascetic discipline of purification. Despite these differences, the mystery religions have some common features. They make no social distinctions; the power of the saving divinities is extended equally to the king,

---

[1] The idea was later exploited by Anaximander, Anaximenes, Heraclitus, Empedocles, and the Stoics.

the peasant and the slave. Every initiate must undergo some form of union with or identification with a god; this is only reasonable, because identification with an immortal confers immortality. Moreover, the gods of the mysteries are immortal in a special sense; Persephone and Dionysus die and are reborn, just as their human worshippers die and are reborn. The nature and essence of the principle of life, the psyche, which is shared by human beings and for that matter by every living thing with these immortal divine powers, rapidly becomes a new center of human interest and curiosity.

The mystery religions, which had thus made the passive acceptance of old traditions about the nature of life henceforth impossible, offered their own solutions of this new problem. The Eleusinian ritual, which consisted of things "done," "shown," and "said," is still obscurely known, and seems to have kept its solution of the problem on the level of action and of feeling.[2] The Orphic solution was far more intellectual; there were many versions of it, and it is impossible to say what precise forms their doctrine had assumed in the seventh century. We know that they told the history of the universe in such a way as to explain the presence of good and evil, and that they represented the nature of life or psyche as identical with Dionysus-Zagreus-Zeus. The psyche, being enclosed in an evil body of divine (Titanic) origin, must be purified in order to secure its happiness; and the penalty of failure was an unhappy immortality or hell.

The Orphic doctrines amply demonstrate that the name of "Zeus" may, in the seventh century, be treated as a mere symbol enclosing a given quantity and quality of divine power, transferable at will to another similar symbol called Dionysus or Zagreus.[3] The Orphics also agree with the ruling

[2] The ritual seems to have conferred immortality by means of sympathetic magic, originally derived from practices which were designed to enhance fertility.

[3] As Paul Monceaux said (s. v. Orphici, Daremberg et Saglio): "all these so-called Orphic gods were merely different names, or various forms, or successive incarnations, of one single god."

Greek belief that one divine power is the source of the universe; and they carry that belief a step further by identifying the divine source with the actual divine universe. The only blots on this unity are the story of the rebellious Titans, and the concept of "body," which is now contrasted as an evil with the good psyche, because "body" is the product of the Titans and like them rebels against the good. Thus the Orphics offered a new and attractive solution of the problem of evil, which through Pythagoras and Plato, as well as through the opponents of this solution, did much to determine the future course of philosophy.

The nature and meaning of "god" (θεός) had thus become one of the most important of all issues for the Greek world of the seventh century B.C. The divine powers called "gods" had not been, even in the time of Homer, invariably represented or conceived as anthropomorphic; and we have seen that the principal basis of the anthropomorphic stories told by Homer was the cult of heroes and the consequent necessity of relating gods to human beings by marriage. But the Greeks of the seventh century felt themselves remote from the time of the heroes, and they were already adopting a new method, and a more "democratic" method, of relating themselves to divine power. In the last three hundred years, they had put forth an intense effort in every field of economic, political, social, religious, intellectual and artistic activity. They had established many prosperous colonies in foreign lands; trade had grown and property systems had been deliberately revolutionized; the city-states had driven out their kings and had begun to overthrow the oligarchs; the conception of a common Hellenic race had been fostered by the epic poets, by the Olympic games, and by the oracle at Delphi; a new national style of Greek art had been formed; and the spirit of investigation, the desire to ascertain and to express facts (called by the Ionians ἱστορίη) was rapidly enriching Greek knowledge of the past, creating new theories and altering old beliefs. Under these circumstances, the

Greeks were beginning to be conscious that every human being possessed power, and in accordance with their firm belief that power was "god" and was divine, they affirmed that a portion of god was in every human being.

The divine power thus present in every man, which was his life and his immortality, was traditionally conceived as a substance, and whatever form it might be imagined to wear after death, no Greek thought of it as anthropomorphic during earthly life.[4] The great motive force behind the anthropomorphic stories of the gods diminished, and the old idea of man's kinship with human gods began to be replaced by the newer idea of man's participation in a divine substance. The Greeks of this period had vivid imaginations, and they have been accused of repeating primitive stories about the gods; but none of them could imagine that the divine substance, of which man's psyche was made, was human in form. They believed that psyche was breath ($\pi\nu\epsilon\hat{\nu}\mu\alpha$); they knew that this substance was invisible, at least ordinarily, and that even the small portion of it in a man had the divine power of life and death over his body. Naturally and inevitably, they began to apply their beliefs about psyche in man to every other living thing; for to live and to have psyche are synonymous.[5] The gods were alive, and the universe was alive; every history of the genesis of the gods, or theogony, was also a history of the genesis of the universe, or cosmogony. In every theogony or cosmogony, various living divine powers were identified with various substances. During the telling of these histories, by a contradiction which is inherent in every narrative, the gods had often been represented in anthropomorphic guise; even a chemist is anthropomorphizing, in a mild and guileless way, when he says that hydrogen and oxygen "combine" to produce water. Nevertheless, the chemist is giving us, in his short narrative, a rational explanation of water; and in pre-

---

[4] "Soul" is a very inadequate rendering of ψυχή (psyche): ψυχή refers to life itself, and to the substance of life, rather than to a "principle" of life.
[5] "Alive," in Greek, is ἔμψυχος.

cisely the same way the theogonist who says that Chaos produced Earth, and that Earth and Sky combined to produce
most of the other gods, has given us a rational explanation of
the gods. A seventh century Greek was just as familiar with
Earth and Sky as we are with oxygen and hydrogen. He regarded them as substances, as we regard the elements; the
only difference is that he thought Earth and Sky were alive
and were filled with divine power. Traditional theogonies,
in spite of the contempt with which many historians dismiss
them, were rational up to a certain point; and now, with the
appearance of doctrines that established a direct connection
between the substance of the life in man and the substance of
the life in the universe, theogony was upon the verge of what
is conventionally known and saluted as the beginning of
philosophy, and as the beginning of rational science.

CHAPTER V

THE BIRTH OF PHILOSOPHY

MANY philosophers, inspired by natural and harmless pride in the achievements of the man whom they recognize as the founder of their profession, represent the birth of philosophy as a kind of miracle. According to them, Thales the Milesian suddenly shook himself free from the bonds of myth and legend, from the irrational theogonies and cosmogonies current in the seventh century, and created philosophy. The histories of philosophy furnish us with an amazing list of the things that Thales was the first to do. He is said to have been the first to institute any general inquiry into the natural causes of things, the first to transfer the World-Stuff from the realm of poetry and mystical feeling and vague conjecture to the realm of everyday fact, the first to grasp the idea of natural regularity, the first to substitute reasons for mere narrative, the first who can rightly be called a man of science, the first to ask and to answer the question whether everything can be regarded as a single reality appearing in different forms. Thales himself has thus become a mythical figure, and the gradual processes of history are cancelled in order to make room for a new legend, which is the legend of Thales.

These enthusiastic characterizations of Thales are misleading in two respects: they build an impenetrable wall around those activities of the human mind that we are entitled to call philosophic or scientific, and they ignore the essential continuity of Greek thought about god. The minds of men are not really divisible into separate bundles of philosophic and scientific thought and vague poetical feeling; "strong men

[38]

lived before Agamemnon," and the poets of Greece had done much to explain the universe to man before Thales appeared. Rational thought remains rational in whatever medium it finds utterance. The contrast between myth and reason is the same sort of false contrast. All depends upon who tells the myth; if he intends to convey a rational meaning, the myth becomes an attempt at history. Of course, if a scholar insists upon using these words as mere terms of abuse, he is well within his rights; and we have no quarrel with him, provided he make his meaning clear. But it is worth while to remember that a myth told by Homer or Hesiod or by a philosopher like Plato belongs in a different category from myths told by ignorant savages. Even now, there is much so-called history in active circulation, eagerly read and studied by educated men, which is far more fictitious than the novels of Thackeray or of Flaubert.

The continuity of Greek thought about god has been obscured by hiding the doctrines of Thales and of his immediate successors under the twin labels of philosophy and science. It is quite true that Thales was a philosopher and a scientist; it is equally true that he was a theologian. Under the influence of modern prepossessions, we habitually regard these three vocations as distinct and to a considerable extent mutually exclusive; but they were combined in Thales as well as in most of his successors, and unless we realize that fact the subsequent development of Greek thought tends to become unintelligible. In this connection, we must add the concepts "natural" and "supernatural" to the list of false antitheses. The Greeks of the time of Thales thought that everything in the universe, including the gods, was natural. Thales asked the question: What substance has the best claim to be looked upon as the living and divine substance which generates the universe out of itself? The question was not wholly new, any more than the answer was wholly new. When Thales proclaimed that Water was the living and divine substance of the universe, the real novelty lay in the fact that there were now, in the sixth century B.C., a number of Greeks who were ready to devote their best energies to the task of discovering a correct solution to this one problem, and in the fact that the supreme divine power was now expressly identified with the cosmogenetic divine substance. They did not eliminate the idea of god from their solutions, but they were primarily interested in a non-anthropomorphic divinity. They did not dream of denying other gods, but they did contribute to the rapid decline of other gods; the divine substance of the universe was obviously more important, they felt, than any god who was a mere creature. Hence they became specialists in the kindred problems of life, of the cosmogenetic god, and of the substance of the universe; and it is the fact of their specialization in these problems that entitles them to be called philosophers.

The scientific achievements of Thales and his followers were very remarkable, particularly in mathematics and astronomy, but they are not directly relevant to the history of the nature and meaning of god. If we bear in mind that the so-called physical doctrines of the Ionian philosophers were really to a great extent metaphysical,[1] we shall be able to understand why the Ionians named one substance after another as the divine source of the universe, without waiting to go through the sober and painstaking process of preliminary investigation that we should expect and demand of a modern physicist before he made an announcement of a new physical theory about the structure of the universe. The Ionians in this respect exemplify the failing which is common to all theorists, including many philosophers and many scientists, who have become fonder of theory than of facts; they venerated a fact only when it was convenient to their special purpose. And since philosophers have laid so much stress upon their claim to rationality, which they will consent to share only with scientists, they must not complain if we take this

---

[1] That is to say, these Greek philosophers believed that they were investigating, and had discovered, the nature of ultimate divine reality, and not of mere outer appearances.

opportunity to point out that the consequences of preferring theory to fact are visible throughout the history of Greek philosophy.

The achievements of Greek philosophers are quite great enough without resorting to exaggeration. No form of human progress is more precarious than progress in what might be termed good sense or reasonableness; and the enthusiastic assertions that with the early Ionian philosophies we pass from a region of twilight mists to "the clarity of sceptical intellect" are only partly justified. The rationality of these philosophers was qualified and limited by many failings, but above all by their intense conviction that each of them possessed an exclusive revelation of the ultimate truth and the ultimate reality. The philosophers will follow the *logos* (argument or reason), as Socrates said, "whithersoever it leads them," and we shall see that it often leads them into strange places. Philosophers have been inclined to contrast themselves with artists, and to find the advantage in point of reasonableness upon their own side; but if we try to be impartial we shall remember that the poet, who portrays human life, frequently knows more about his subject than the philosopher, who explains the universe, knows about the universe.

Thales was undoubtedly influenced by Homeric tradition in his statement that Water was the divine source of all things and the living substance of the universe. We do not know what technical vocabulary Thales employed; he may have called this non-anthropomorphic god the genesis (as Homer did), the physis ($\phi \acute{\upsilon} \sigma \iota \varsigma$), or the arche ($\dot{\alpha} \rho \chi \acute{\eta}$) of all things. It is certain, however, that he said that "all things are full of living divine powers," and that "even a magnetic stone has Life (Psyche), because it moves iron." When these statements are considered in their relation to the problems we know he was investigating, they become quite intelligible, and there is no need to doubt the approximate correctness of Aristotle's inferences: Aristotle interpreted the first statement to mean that "Life (Psyche) is diffused throughout the universe," and the second to mean that "Life (Psyche) is a source of motion."[2] It is entirely possible that Aristotle was drawing upon some trustworthy tradition when he suggested that Thales was influenced not only by the old belief about Okeanos in his choice of Water as the divine substance, but also by more practical considerations. The passage in the *Metaphysics* (983b) runs as follows: "Thales, the founder of this school of philosophy, says the first cause is Water (for which reason he declared that the earth rests on Water), getting the notion perhaps from seeing that the nutriment of all things is moist, and that heat itself is generated from the moist and kept alive by it (and that from which they come to be is a first cause of all things). He got his notion from this fact, and from the fact that the seeds of all things have a moist nature, and that water is the origin of the nature (or substance) of moist things." Modern scholars, who imagined that Thales was talking not about a living divine substance but about a "material" cause, and who therefore failed to see the relevance of nutriment, heat, and seeds to the source of Life, have invented meteorological reasons for the choice of Water, such as evaporation, and the rivers with their alluvial deposits. These reasons are interesting enough in themselves; but they have nothing to do with Thales and his inquiry into the source of Life. The supreme god, and the cosmogenetic god, were one divine power, Water; and Thales supported his choice of Water by strictly appropriate arguments. Nutriment is moist; therefore Water is the source of all growth: heat (akin to Fire) is produced from and maintained by the moist; therefore Water is the source of all Fire: the seeds of all things are moist; therefore Water is the source of all Life.

Anaximander, the pupil of Thales, was born in 610/9 B.C.,

---

[2] *De Anima*, 411 a 7; 405 a 19. Aristotle's interpretation is only approximately correct, because he failed to include the attribute of divinity along with the Psyche that is diffused through all things: he thus left the way open to those modern historians who have eliminated god from early Greek philosophy, and have reduced this and similar doctrines to "hylozoism" or "panpsychism." It is not merely Life that is diffused; it is divine Life, a genuine creative force.

and died in 546/5. Dissatisfied with the choice that his master had made, he characterized the cosmogenetic god as the Infinite and Indeterminate (one word in the Greek— ἄπειρον) first cause, "from which all the skies and the universes within them come to be."[3] This substance is "immortal and imperishable," and therefore it is "the divine power" (τὸ θεῖον) that "contains all things and steers all things."[4] This Infinite and Indeterminate god engenders finite and determinate substances such as fire and air, earth and water, day and night. Anaximander accounts for the unending succession of changes in the universe by representing these "opposites" (ἐναντιό-τητες) as mortal and subject to decay: "according to necessity all things that exist pass away into that from which they come into being; for they pay each other the just penalty for their wrongdoing according to their order in time."[5] That is to say, fire "does wrong" to air and becomes air, water "does wrong" to earth and becomes earth, night "does wrong" to day and becomes day, and vice versa. These opposite and perishable substances are separated out of the one imperishable substance that is the Infinite and Indeterminate; and they undergo, in accordance with divine Necessity, which resembles Moira, a continuous process of birth and death that is exactly parallel to the "circle of birth" (κύκλος γενέσεως) of Orphic and Pythagorean doctrine.

What has happened to the god of Thales? Anaximander pays deliberate tribute to divine Water, in what has been called his "crowning audacity," his theory of the origin of animals: "living creatures are dried out of moist vapor by the sun; man was in the beginning like another animal, i.e. a fish." Water and Fire are the source of life. On the other hand, Anaximander agrees with his successor, Anaximenes, that the specific substance of life is Air. The ease with which these lesser divine substances change their names and forms is extremely disconcerting to our minds, but is in complete

[3] *FV*, 2, 9.   [5] *ibid.*, 2, 9.
[4] *ibid.*, 2, 15.

accord with Greek habits of thought about the divine power; the Greeks used different words to refer to slightly different aspects of the same divine power, with no more feeling that they violated the rules of reason than when they used the name of Zeus to refer to the sky, the weather, or to destiny. But there is a genuine novelty in the name and nature of Anaximander's supreme deity. The idea of god has begun its long journey away from the notion of substance and towards the notion of "pure" causality. This supreme god is still a substance, but it is no longer a namable and definite substance like Water.

Anaximander had observed that every namable and definite substance "perishes" and becomes its own opposite; these perishable substances are close kin, since they are separated out of the supreme god, but they are subordinate and inferior. They are in fact analogous to the mystery gods like Dionysus and Persephone, and to the Psychai (Souls) of their human worshippers, still immortal, but with a qualified immortality that permits them to perish and to be born again. Therefore Anaximander emphasizes the indeterminateness of his supreme god; to be indeterminate is to be free from the process of change except in so far as a cause is not "free" from its result. The infinity of Anaximander's supreme god is due to the fact that he regards the process of change as unending, and the cause of an unending process must be inexhaustible.[6] The supreme god has also begun to be located outside the mutable universes which it enfolds (περιέχει);[7] its function as an envelope which is the source of all life and change within the universe or the universes is Anaximander's version of an idea which reappears in many Greek philosophies, not only in the Air of Anaximenes but in the infinite Fire of Heraclitus and the "membrane" of which Leucippus speaks, and which is still recognizable in the location of the supreme god of Aristotle.

[6] *FV*, 2, 14: ἵνα μηδὲν ἐλλείπῃ ἡ γένεσις — "in order that the source of becoming may not fail."
[7] *ibid.*, 2, 11.

Anaximenes, who flourished about 546/5 B.C., was the pupil and associate of Anaximander, and accepted his master's theology in every respect but one. He agreed that the cosmogenetic god was the Infinite and Indeterminate, but he asserted against Anaximander that it was a definite and namable substance.[8] Anaximenes said that "infinite and indeterminate Air was the first cause, and that out of it come all things present, past, and future, and gods and things divine; and all else comes to be from the offspring of Air":[9] and that "just as our Life (Psyche) being Air, has sovereign power over us, so Pneuma and Air contains [sic] the entire universe."[10] How can we understand the paradox of a supreme god who is at once definite and infinite and indeterminate ($\dot{\omega}\rho\iota\sigma\mu\acute{\epsilon}\nu\sigma$ and $\check{\alpha}\pi\epsilon\iota\rho\sigma$)?

Anaximenes did not intend a paradox; he was merely continuing the family quarrel which had begun with his master. Anaximander had criticized Thales for proposing as a supreme god a substance which according to Anaximander was neither infinite nor indeterminate; since Water was not indeterminate, he argued that it was exposed to change, and was constantly perishing into its opposite. Now Anaximenes intervened in the debate. He asserted that he could name a substance which was qualitatively indeterminate, but which was also the source of every qualitative determination. Divine Air could change into everything else, and yet retain its identity; and Anaximenes explained this apparent miracle by introducing the devices of rarefaction and condensation. In this way Air remained indeterminate, but was also namable and definite. The changes which take place in the universe are no longer as real as they were even in the system of Anaximander; and the supreme god has taken another step on the path which led from the status of substance or of "stuff" to

---

[8] FV, 3 A 5.　　　　　　　[9] ibid., 3 A 7.
[10] ibid., 3 B 2: οἶον ἡ ψυχὴ ἡ ἡμετέρα ἀὴρ οὖσα συγκρατεῖ ἡμᾶς, καὶ ὅλον τὸν κόσμον πνεῦμα καὶ ἀὴρ περιέχει. Πνεῦμα and ἀήρ are treated as the singular subject of περιέχει.

the status of pure cause. Air is less substantial than the Apeiron, and the Apeiron is less substantial than Water.

It is interesting to note that as the supreme god travels upward in the scale of substances, in obedience to the philosophic and theological quest for a definition of god which should more nearly approach perfection than any preceding definition, this god has now reached the point of being expressly identified with Air and Pneuma, which Greek tradition had always asserted to be the stuff of the Psyche. The two terms are practically synonymous; Pneuma differs from Air only because it is a rarefied form of Air, and resembles the subtlest form of Air, which is Fire. Thus Anaximenes has consecrated in his philosophy the popular belief of the Greeks concerning the substantial cause of life, which under the names of Fire or Pneuma will play a central part in the speculation of Heraclitus, the Pythagoreans, and the Stoics, and which is familiar in later times as the divine Spirit.

The philosophy of Anaximenes is of course also a theogony. He disposes of all other gods in summary fashion; they are mere transformations of the supreme god Air. Their existence is not denied or doubted; as Saint Augustine says, "nec deos negavit ant tacuit, non tamen ab ipsis aerem factum, sed ipsos ex aere ortos credidit."[11] These gods did not "create" Air; they arise out of Air. But their rank is conspicuously reduced, and they have sunk to the status of temporal metamorphoses of the one eternal Arche or Physis. In the theology of Anaximenes, there are in reality no longer any anthropomorphic gods; all gods are aeromorphic. We shall see that the procedure of Anaximenes is imitated by all subsequent Greek philosophers who still think that the lesser gods are worth explaining.

[11] *FV*, 3 A 10.

CHAPTER VI

PYTHAGORAS

WHILE the Milesian school were quietly debating the nature of the supreme divine power, Pythagoras, a contemporary of Anaximander and of Anaximenes, demonstrated the ease with which such studies may be converted into a passionate and bewildering mixture of religion, philosophy, and science.[1] The central purpose of Pythagoras was to purify the Psyche of man and to guarantee a happy immortality by a special discipline, and in so far the religion of Pythagoras resembles the Orphic mysteries. But there was a vital difference between the mind of an ordinary Orphic initiate, whose curiosity concerning the universe was quenched by a few simple doctrines, and the mind of Pythagoras, who worshipped knowledge and wisdom ($\sigma o\phi i a$) as the source of salvation. The pursuit of wisdom therefore acquired a new meaning. To Pythagoras and to the greatest of his followers, the study and contemplation of the universe was the supreme religious duty of man; it was the means by which man could become like god. Pythagoras, like Plato, subordinated philosophy to his hope of salvation; and al-

---

[1] The texts upon which this chapter is based are nearly all to be found in Zeller. But the views of Zeller, which have been in large measure adopted by other historians, led him to minimize or to deny the intimate connection between the religious doctrines and the philosophic doctrines of the early Pythagoreans, and also led him to deny the authenticity of much of the available evidence about Pythagoras and his early followers. This sceptical attitude has been rendered impossible, and the whole study of early Pythagoreanism has been revolutionized, by the brilliant and essentially sound works of Augusto Rostagni and of Armand Delatte, to whom the history of Greek philosophy owes a great debt. These scholars are of course not in the least responsible for errors in my interpretation of early Pythagoreanism. I have tried to limit this interpretation to doctrines which may now be reasonably ascribed to Pythagoras himself.

though, as Heraclitus says, "Pythagoras, son of Mnesarchus, worked out his inquiry (ἱστορίην) more elaborately than all other men,"[2] the end that he had in view was not disinterested, or at least not wholly disinterested.

The results of his attempt to turn philosophy into a mystery religion are manifest in all that is known of his life and of his doctrines. As a prophet of god and a spokesman of Apollo, his faith in his own partial divinity was infectious; during his life he made hundreds of converts in Magna Graecia, to whom he offered the privileges of an ascetic discipline and the promise that their immortal Psychai, being gradually purified, should ascend into "the uppermost region" in which the gods dwelt. As a philosopher and theologian, he occupied himself with the problems of life, of the cosmogenetic god, and of the substance of the universe, and he stated these problems in about the same terms that the Milesians had employed, with the one important exception of his mathematical doctrines.

Pythagoras was dissatisfied, as Anaximenes had been dissatisfied, with the Infinite and Indeterminate god of Anaximander; and like Anaximenes he asserted against Anaximander the claims of a definite and namable divine substance. Anaximenes had proposed divine Air as the one cause of all apparent diversity in the universe; Pythagoras, working thus far along the same line of thought, proposed divine Fire as the cosmogenetic god, the source of immortal life and the substance of the universe. And then Pythagoras identified the divine Fire with the divine One, and by this puzzling identification of substance with number caused endless trouble to all who attempt to understand Pythagoreanism without being Pythagoreans. If we were within the circle of his

---

[2] Diogenes Laertius, VIII, 6. See Delatte's edition, *La vie de Pythagore de Diogène Laërce*, 159 *ff.*, for the history of the controversy about the genuineness of this fragment of Heraclitus. It was rejected by Diels, but Gercke very ably established its authenticity in the *Einleitung in die Altertumswissenschaft*, II[3], 459: and Delatte accepts Gercke's results. It is not however probable that ἱστορίην means "das vorhandene Wissen anderer": with this exception, I accept Gercke's interpretation.

thought and his passions, if we were members of his church ($\sigma\upsilon\nu\acute{\epsilon}\delta\rho\iota\upsilon\nu$) at Croton, we should be likely to have some inner understanding of what the master meant by saying that the universe was made of numbers and that the divine One was the source of all numbers, and even if we failed to understand we should as converts find the doctrine easy to accept. There is perhaps some consolation in the fact that Aristotle, whose own master was an authentic intellectual heir of Pythagoras, found the doctrine very difficult.

The mystery may be diminished if not solved, if we bear in mind the principle which operated in Homer: the possession of power generates the Greek gods. Pythagoras attributed divinity to One, because the One seemed to him to have inexhaustible power and was therefore like the Infinite and Indeterminate of Anaximander, and because the One was also the source of all determination and limitation, both in the cosmic process and in the series of numbers which was generated precisely as the universe was generated. It is easy enough for us to understand how Pythagoras arrived at the conclusion that the One has divine power over a series of numbers; the One contains in itself both the odd and the even numbers. And we can see an analogy between the power of Anaximander's Apeiron over the universe and the power of the divine One over the odd and the even numbers; these numbers are derived from the One, and are "opposites," just as the opposites air and fire, day and night, are separated out of the Apeiron. Moreover, these opposite numbers are subject to change; the odd passes into or is transformed into the even as air changes into fire. But these analogies between the behavior of the One and the behavior of the Apeiron, together with the undoubted fact that Pythagoras believed the One to be the supreme god, still leave us in partial obscurity. How could Pythagoras, fascinated as he must have been by newly acquired mathematical knowledge, have ventured to fancy that a number was a god? Granting that the possession of power made a Greek god, how can Pythagoras have imagined that the One had power over anything but numbers? We might admit that the One could have been thought of as a little mathematical god. But how could a mathematical god have made the universe?

These intellectual difficulties, which have been felt by most students of Pythagoreanism, are due to the fact that we involuntarily ask the wrong questions; we insist upon treating as a puzzle a doctrine of god which was not intended as a puzzle, but as an explanation. The question should not be "How can a number be a god?" but "If the One is the supreme god, with what does Pythagoras intend to contrast the One?" Here at last we have a question to which an intelligible answer can be given. The obvious contrast to the One is the many, τὸ πλῆθος or τὰ πολλά in Greek; and "the many" is the regular expression employed by Greek philosophers to signify the multitude of diverse things in the universe. The Pythagorean One is not a mere number; it is an affirmation of divine causal Unity set against the plurality of changing things within the cosmos. When Pythagoras asserted that the supreme god was the One, he did not in the least intend to deny that the supreme god was Fire and was the source of all life and of the universe; he accepted all these beliefs, and sought to improve the definition of the supreme god, thus obtained, by emphasizing his conviction that the supreme god was also the One and the source of all unity, as well as the first cause of all numbers and the determining principle in all diversity.

From this point of view, the doctrine of the One is not quite so enigmatic. If we are willing to make the attempt, we may replace ourselves by an effort of sympathy within reach of the conviction that generated this doctrine. We shall then see the One as a sphere of Fire or Aither, surrounding that which is to be the cosmos, and also situated at the centre of that sphere, since "the most important part of the cosmos, which is the centre, should be most strictly guarded"; and to this central Fire we shall give various other names, besides that of the One.[3] It will be the Sentinel of Zeus; it will be the Mother of the gods, because it will produce the gods which we see as the Stars, the five Planets, the Sun, the Moon, the Earth and the counter-Earth, which we shall invent because we must have another god to complete the divine number Ten, also known as the Tetraktys of the Decad; and we shall also call it the divine Hearth-fire (Hestia, cf. Philolaus, *FV*, 32 A 16) and the Keel ($\tau\rho\acute{o}\pi\iota s$, *FV*, 32 A 17) of the universe, just as we call the sphere of enveloping Fire or Aither the Hull or Ship ($\acute{o}\lambda\kappa\acute{a}s$, *FV*, 32 B 12) which carries the universe as its freight.[4]

The one Fire will be a Limit (Peras, cf. Aristotle *De Caelo*, 293 a) both at the centre and at all points on the sphere of enveloping Fire; but if we imagine ourselves situated at any point on that sphere and we then look outward beyond the sphere and away from the Unity of that sphere, we shall see a vague stuff extending to infinity in all directions outside the sphere. This vague stuff is full of potentialities; when those potentialities are limited and converted into realities by the One Fire, the One Fire is forming the universe. For this vague stuff, we shall employ the name already made familiar by Anaximander; since it is infinite and indetermi-

---

[3] *FV*, 45 B 37 (Aristotle, *De Caelo*, 293 a 18 *ff*., and the commentary of Simplicius). Some scholars, e.g. Burnet, have argued that this doctrine could not have been part of primitive Pythagoreanism, and that Pythagoras must have believed in a geocentric system. Zeller was undoubtedly right in maintaining that the doctrine of the central Fire belongs to primitive Pythagoreanism. As explained by Aristotle, the doctrine of the counter-Earth belongs to the theory of the Tetraktys of the Decad; and the Decad was certainly invented by Pythagoras. Later Greek philosophers, who believed in a geocentric universe, were reactionary.

The Tetraktys of the Decad represents the divine number 10 as the triangle of 4: see Burnet, *Early Greek Philosophy*[3], 102. The figure would be like this:

. .
. . .
. . . .

[4] For the evidence, derived from Aristotle, Hippasos, and Parmenides, that Pythagoras identified Fire with Limit, cf. Burnet, *Early Greek Philosophy*[3], 109. The Metaphors Keel and Hull, applied to the One Fire at the centre and at the periphery of the universe, obviously belong to the same system; and Wilamowitz's conjecture, $\acute{o}\lambda\kappa\acute{o}s$, would destroy this harmony (*Platon*, II, 91, 92). Wilamowitz interprets $\acute{o}\lambda\kappa\acute{o}s$ as the "wrapping" or the "volume" of the sphere.

nate, we shall call it the apeiron. This Pythagorean apeiron no longer deserves the capital letter, since it is no longer the supreme god that it was in the doctrine of Anaximander; but it is the indispensable means which the Pythagorean supreme god must utilize. We shall therefore represent the living divine One as extracting from the apeiron that surrounds it everything necessary for the life and growth and change that go on within its sphere. These necessary materials cannot be enumerated, since they are infinite; but three of the most important can be named. The One is eternal, but within the universe it must employ time; the One is Fire or Aither,[5] but within the universe it needs to employ, for all living creatures, the related but less subtle substance that we know as breath; the One is continuous, if we think of it as the one spherical Fire, but within the universe it needs to employ a principle of discontinuity, that we call the void ($\tau\grave{o}$ $\kappa\epsilon\nu\acute{o}\nu$). Since the One is itself living, we shall think of it as "breathing in" these necessary materials; this is the explanation of the famous passage in the *Physics* (213 b) of Aristotle: "The Pythagoreans also affirmed the existence of the void, and that it entered the Sky from the infinite pneuma,[6] since the Sky breathes in also the void; the void sets a boundary to all things that undergo natural processes, since the void is that which separates consecutive objects and bounds them; this void also exists first of all in numbers, for the void sets a boundary to the nature of numbers."

The living One is now maintaining life and change by breathing in the indeterminate. It thus creates within itself the many. We do not yet know enough to give a detailed account of the cosmic process; that will have to wait for our followers Philolaus and Plato. But we have some knowledge of mathematics, of astronomy, and of animals, including man; and since our own salvation depends to a considerable extent

[5] Aither is merely another name for the subtlest and purest part of Air or Fire.

[6] Reading $\epsilon\pi\epsilon\iota\sigma\iota\acute{\epsilon}\nu\alpha\iota$ $\alpha\grave{v}\tau\hat{\omega}$ $\tau\hat{\omega}$ $o\grave{v}\rho\alpha\nu\hat{\omega}$ $\grave{\epsilon}\kappa$ $\tauo\hat{v}$ $\grave{\alpha}\pi\epsilon\acute{\iota}\rho o\upsilon$ $\pi\nu\epsilon\acute{v}\mu\alpha\tauo\varsigma$, with all the MSS. The conjectures of Diels ($\pi\nu\epsilon\hat{v}\mu\acute{\alpha}$ $\tau\epsilon$) and of Heidel ($\pi\nu\epsilon\hat{v}\mu\alpha$) are unnecessary.

PYTHAGORAS

upon our using the little knowledge we have, in order to ensure the purification of our Souls and our happy immortality, we shall make a desperate attempt to stretch out what we know until it covers the cosmos. Our supreme god is the one Fire; the Stars, the Planets, and the Sun are clearly of kindred fire, and are the principal subordinate gods; they dwell in a purer region, where there is less change and life is more nearly perfect.[7] The moon is intermediate in virtue, but is better than the Earth. Here on Earth we men are imprisoned, being surrounded by bodies, by constant change and imperfection; but we have Life (Psyche) within us, and are therefore akin to the One Fire. The purest part of the Life or Soul within us is mind or reason, and we may speak of it as a fragment of the One which is the source of all order ($\kappa\acute{o}\sigma\mu o\varsigma$.[8])

Through our study of mathematics and of music, we have made some discoveries about number and harmonic intervals; and we promptly seize upon them and exalt them into explanations of the order which is due to the One as it works upon the indeterminate. The One produces the many particular things; and not only man but every particular thing shows forth the handiwork of the One, since the One, in producing it, has arranged it in a particular order, and not only man but everything in the universe is a microcosm, a cosmos on a small scale, contained within the one cosmos which is on a large scale. As Pythagoreans, we believe that each of these many microcosms can be expressed or explained or defined in terms of number; since the One, besides being the supreme god, is the supreme source of unity, and in each microcosm the One has exerted its action upon a certain definite amount of the indeterminate.[9] The One is the supreme number, and "a certain definite amount of the indeterminate," which has been made definite and converted into an orderly unity by the One,

[7] cf. Diogenes Laertius, VIII, 26, and the commentary of Delatte (p. 206): "It is the perpetual movement of the Air that determines its purity, its aptitude to form and to preserve life."
[8] Diogenes Laertius, VIII, 28: "The Psyche is a fragment of Aither."
[9] cf. Aristotle, *Metaphysics*, 987 a 9 ff.

[53]

is also a number. By study and by θεωρία (active contemplation), which are the means of our salvation, we believe that we can find out the actual number which in each case represents that certain definite amount of the indeterminate; and the number so ascertained will seem to us to be the very inner secret of the thing itself, to be the essence of the thing, since the number will in each case reveal to us exactly what the supreme god meant when he made that particular microcosm. We have the advantage over later mathematicians that we are possessed by religious faith, as well as by the normal conviction of absolute certitude which inspires all mathematicians and all who lean heavily upon logic; and because we have religious faith we know what we are talking about, while later mathematicians will merely be certain that their reasoning is correct, and will not know at all to what their reasoning refers.

We Pythagoreans can therefore say that all things are numbers, and we shall quite reasonably (from our point of view) come to the most fantastic conclusions; and we shall not hesitate to assign numbers to things which later will appear to be abstractions, but are to us real essences. Thus we shall say that justice is four or nine (the first square numbers), that marriage is five, and that the divine Tetraktys of the Decad is the most binding oath, since the Tetraktys has within it the Source and Root of ever-flowing Nature (παγὰν ἀενάου φύσεως ῥίζωμά τ' ἔχουσαν, Iamblichus, V. P., 150, 162).[10]

Since it is the One that creates order in each particular thing and group of things, from the Psyche to the city-state and the universe, by combining with itself some definite amount of the apeiron, we shall search for a term to designate the function of the One as a combining agent, and we shall choose the word ἁρμονία. This word means a "binding"; Homer has used it of the clamps or joints that Odysseus used in building his raft (Od., V, 248). Since every binding made

[10] On the Tetraktys, see the indispensable study of Delatte, *Etudes sur la littérature pythagoricienne*, 249-68.

by the One is orderly, we shall use ἁρμονία either in its active sense as "that which binds and produces order" or in its passive sense as "that which is bound into order." We are acquainted with such musical intervals as the octave, the fifth, and the fourth, and with the mathematical proportions which correspond to these intervals; but the word Harmonia will always mean a binding, whether or not it refers to a concordant sound or a ratio. The most splendid Harmonia is that of the divine Stars and Planets, which revolve swiftly in ten circular orbits, and produce by their swift motion a sound of marvellous beauty; but mortals cannot hear this music, or else mortals hear it and cannot distinguish it because they have always heard it.[11]

Our souls, which now bind our bodies into order, are immortal; but the portion of the One that they contain is too feeble to make this binding permanent. Its dissolution is the "release" (λύσις) of death. After the Psyche is released, it enters into another body (metensomatosis), higher or lower in the scale of life according to the purity of the Psyche's conduct and its success in following and making itself like unto the one supreme god, who is perfect purity. Every entrance of the Psyche into a body is a punishment inflicted by the one supreme god, and resembles entrance into a tomb or a prison; if the Psyche fails in purity, it may be sent into the body of a lower animal, and if its failure be grave, it will undergo especial punishment in Hades. During this desperate struggle for purity, the gods are our keepers and we are their prisoners and wards. Occasionally, some vague divine power (τὸ δαιμόνιον) or daimon will intervene in our life. "The whole air is full of Psychai, which are called daimons and heroes; they send men dreams and signs of disease and health, and not only to men but to sheep and cattle also; to them purifications,

---

[11] Aristotle, *De Caelo*, 290 b 12 *ff*. The translation of ἁρμονία as "harmony," even with reference to the music of the spheres, is incorrect and misleading; the music that the spheres produce is the result of their being bound together in a definite mathematical combination.

propitiatory sacrifices, and all divination and omens and the like have reference" (*Diogenes Laertius*, VIII, 32).

In the midst of these gratifying beliefs, which are integral with our philosophy, we shall remember that when our master Pythagoras descended into Hades, he saw the Soul of Hesiod bound to a pillar of bronze and uttering little shrill cries, and the Soul of Homer hanging from a tree and surrounded by serpents, in punishment for what they had said about the gods. Stesichorus was merely blinded for his attack upon the goddess Helen; we are already employing the threat of damnation against those poets who attribute to the gods conduct that we regard as impure. Except for this doctrine of the purity of the gods, we shall accept, in the name of the love of wisdom, all the ordinary religious beliefs and practices of our fellow Greeks; we shall use the lesser gods, in strict accordance with our philosophy, as the divine inhabitants of the corners of various cubes and other geometrical figures.[12] But in comparison with the One Fire, all other gods will sink into insignificance.

If at this point we abandon the pretence that we are Pythagoreans, and turn back upon this brief summary of the most essential doctrines of Pythagoras, we see at once that the character of the supreme god is changing away from substance towards causality, in the same general direction that is followed by the supreme gods of Anaximander and Anaximenes. The One is the most powerful of all causes; it is so to speak progressively withdrawing itself from substance, although it still clings to Fire and Aither. It does not grow, but it is the cause of growth. It does not change, but it is the cause of change. In the realm of numbers, there is an apparent exception to this last statement. The One seems to be the source, as well as the cause, of all numbers; but clearly the familiar concept of growth is hardly applicable to mathematical processes. And yet the One is in some sense the source of the number two as well as of all other even num-

[12] cf. Zeller, I, 1⁷, 499.

bers; and even numbers partake of the nature of the apeiron. Can the One itself have a double nature? In the long history of metaphysics, the logical difficulty that must be faced by those who would reconcile the oneness of the supreme cause with the diversity of that which it causes has brought forth innumerable attempted solutions. Pythagoras himself was probably too much occupied with his contrast between the One and the many to feel the difficulty acutely. He was satisfied with the device of Harmonia. But Philolaus, Plato and all later Pythagoreans were driven more and more to emphasize the changeableness and the unreality of the many; and since a perfect cause is inappropriate to an imperfect result, they accentuated the partial and unsystematic dualism of Pythagoras.

The dualism of Pythagoras is only partial, because he set the active One above the comparatively passive many, and not on the same level with them. But when he dealt with the Psyche of man, and its imprisonment in the body, and the possibility of its release from the body and from the circle of becoming (κύκλος γενέσεως), his very detestation of the body forced him to assign to it a status practically coordinate with that of the Psyche. It seems to be the fate of ascetics to exaggerate the importance of that which they detest; hatred and good sense refuse to live together, even in the mind of a philosopher. His hostility to the body did not prevent him from encouraging gymnastics; but it did lead him to the verge of open conflict with the old belief in anthropomorphic gods. The only substance fitting for a god was Fire or Air; the only activity fitting for a god was pure causal activity. Pythagoras could not therefore put into effect his doctrine of the purity of the Psyche and of the gods, as long as the minds of men accepted the stories of anthropomorphic gods as straightforward true accounts. In the name of purity, of theology and of philosophy he declared war on the poets; and human intelligence has not yet proved adequate to the task of making peace. In making war upon the poets, Pythagoras prudently limited himself to damning the Souls of Homer and Hesiod and to the composition of anthologies of their poetry, from which he doubtless omitted all the heretical and impure passages; the poets had too secure a hold upon the affections of the Greeks to permit of their abolition, and Pythagoras seems actually to have favored the study of the orthodox anthologies as a means of purifying the Psyche. He is said to have enjoyed singing, to his own accompaniment, the verses in which Homer describes the death of Euphorbus, the Phrygian whose body was inhabited by the Psyche of Pythagoras at the time of the Trojan War.[13]

The power of Pythagoras and his influence upon subsequent theological and philosophical thought can hardly be overestimated. It is not merely that his emphasis upon form and limit and the numerical essence of things is the prelude to the Parmenidean and to the Leucippean and the Platonic doctrines of Forms; his worship of the supreme One was the direct parent of the doctrines of Xenophanes and of the whole Eleatic school. Above all, his peculiar combination of mathematical certainty and logic with the passionate search for purity of the Psyche was bound to engender both the spirit and the theory of intolerance and of persecution, of orthodoxy and of heresy. It is not surprising that his disciples at Croton, who had acquired political power, finally roused such opposition that many of them were burned in the church which was their place of assembly, and that the Pythagoreans, as an organized political power, were everywhere broken up. It is not surprising that Plato, who learned much from Pythagoras, should have written both the *Apology* in defence of the persecuted and the *Laws*, which contain a defence of persecution.

[13] See Delatte's excellent essay upon the Pythagorean exegesis of Homer, in his *Etudes sur la littérature pythagoricienne*, 110 ff.

CHAPTER VII

XENOPHANES

XENOPHANES of Colophon is thought to have been born about 580 B.C.; and we have his own word for it that he was still alive at the age of ninety-two. He was poet, philosopher, and theologian; he had wandered much, and in his old age lived in Elea in southern Italy, and in Zancle (the modern Messina) and Catana (the modern Catania) in Sicily.

Xenophanes was a poet, and not an ascetic, but he had more faith in Pythagoras than in Homer. A few of the fragments of his poetry will reveal his doctrine.

"Men should first cheerfully hymn the god with pious tales and pure speech; then after libation and prayer that we may have strength to do what is right—for that is the simplest of all prayers—it is no excess to drink as much as a man can carry home without an attendant, supposing he be not a very old man. The man who deserves praise is he who, after drinking, sets forth famous deeds, as his memory and his zeal for excellence permit. Let him not sing of the battles of the Titans, the Giants, or the Centaurs, fictions of the men who lived before us, or of violent civil revolts, in which there is nothing honorable; but let him be always mindful of the gods, as is right" (*FV*, 11 B 1).

"Better than the strength of men or of horses is my wisdom" (this is from a poem in dispraise of athletes, *FV*, 11 B 2).

"They say that he [Pythagoras] once came by when a dog was being ill-treated, and that he uttered this saying: 'Stop, beat him no more, for it is the Psyche of a friend of mine, which I recognized when I heard its voice' " (*FV*, 11 B 7).

"Since all men from the beginning have learned according to Homer . . . " (*FV*, 11 B 10).

"Homer and Hesiod have attributed all things to the gods, all things that among men are a source of reproach and blame, stealing, adultery, and deceiving one another. . . . Mortals imagine that the gods are begotten, and that the gods wear clothes like their own, and have voice (or language) and form like the voice and form of mortals. . . . But if oxen and horses or lions had hands or could draw and do the work with their hands that men do, horses would have drawn the forms of gods like horses, and oxen gods like oxen, and they would represent the bodies of the gods as just like their own forms. . . . Ethiopians make their gods snub-nosed and black; Thracians make theirs blue-eyed and red-haired. . . . There is One God, greatest among gods and men, not like mortals in form or in thought. . . . The One God is all sight, and is all thought, and is all hearing. . . . But the One God without effort brandishes all things by the thought of his mind (νόου φρενί). . . . The One God abides ever in the same, never moving; nor is it fitting that he travel now in this direction and now in that" (*FV*, 11 B 11, 14, 15, 16, 23-6).

"The gods have not revealed all things to mortals from the beginning, but by searching mortals find out, in the course of time, that which is better" (*FV*, 11 B 18).

"No man has ever been or ever will be who knows the exact truth about the gods and about that which I say concerning the universe: for even if he should happen to utter the perfect truth, yet he himself does not know it; but opinion is upon all things" (*FV*, 11 B 18).

"Let this opinion be adopted as like the truth" (*FV*, 11 B 35).

"All things come from earth and end in earth. . . . All things that come into being and grow are earth and water. . . . The sea is the source of water and the source of wind. . . . She whom they call Iris is a cloud likewise, purple scarlet and

green to look upon. . . . We are all born of earth and water"
(*FV*, 11 B 27, 29, 30, 32, 33).

Xenophanes is perhaps the best example in the whole history of Greek thought of the extreme rapidity and boldness
with which a Greek would seize upon a tendency, upon an
idea which was in course of development, and convert it into
a full-blown conclusion. We are still in the sixth century B.C.,
and already Xenophanes has taken the supreme god further
along the same path which had led to the Air of Anaximenes
and to the One Fire of Pythagoras; the One God of Xenophanes has reached the point where substance disappears, and
it stands revealed as pure causality and pure unity, unham-
pered by even the subtlest of physical attributes, except that
it "coheres" with all that it causes. With the approximate
disappearance of these attributes, the idea of the supreme god
has attained a crisis in its history. It is true that Xenophanes
was following in general the same direction of thought as
his great contemporaries; nevertheless there is a difference
between climbing a mountain and the moment of arrival upon
the summit, and the fact that Xenophanes had reached the
summit forced him to express his vision of the supreme god
mostly in terms of negation and contradiction. The view
from the top was very different from the view a little below
the top.

On the positive and affirmatory side, Xenophanes declares
that the One God is supreme; it is "greatest among gods and
men," and "brandishes all things by the thought of its mind,"
as befits the supreme cause. Also, the One God is all "sight
and thought and hearing"; it is the supremely active Mind:
and yet it "abides ever in the same." To this brief list of
positive qualities only a few more assertions can be added,
with any degree of plausibility, from the sources: Xenophanes
seems to have said that the One God is "throughout alike"
or "identical" (πανταχόθεν ὅμοιον, *FV*, 11 A 31), that the
One God is "always alike" (ἀεὶ ὅμοιον, *FV*, 11 A 32), and

that the One God is "coherent with" or "attached to" all things (συμφυῆ τοῖς πᾶσιν, *FV*, 11 A 35).

Even among these positive statements, there are several which can only be understood if we replace them in the context of sixth century ideas about the supreme god; and then they turn out to be negations. Anaximenes had allowed his divine Air to be rarefied and condensed; even the divine One of Pythagoras, since it was also Fire, seemed to be a substance capable of change and division, and the Psyche of man was not only akin to all life but was believed to be a "fragment" of the divine Aither. The mystery religions depended upon gods who died and were born again, like their worshippers; and the religious tradition of all Greeks had represented the gods as part of a cosmic history, in the course of which they had successively come into being. Against all these beliefs, Xenophanes set a mark of cancellation; he proclaimed, in the name of the perfection of his One God, that the One God was not thicker here and thinner there, but was alike throughout. The One God could not move about, or be now at the centre of the universe and now at the enclosing sphere, or scattered in fragmentary souls, but was alike throughout. The One God could not die and come into being, nor could any time be imagined when the One God was not or would not be; therefore the One God is always alike, and has passed out of time into eternity, and must be called not "immortal" (ἀθάνατος) but "eternal" (ἀίδιος) and "unbegotten" (ἀγέννητος) and "free from becoming" (ἀγένητος).

In the same way, we can explain two of the apparently startling paradoxes which are reported by Simplicius (*FV*, 11 A 31). "Xenophanes says that the One God is neither infinite and indeterminate nor finite and determinate, since that which does not exist is the infinite and indeterminate, because it has no beginning or middle or end, and since it is the many that limit and determine each other. Similarly, he deprives the One God both of motion and of rest, since that which does not exist is the unmoved, because nothing else ever comes into it nor does it go into anything else; and the things which are moved are those which are more than the one [i.e. 'the many'], for one thing changes into another. And so when Xenophanes says that the One God abides ever in the same, . . . he does not mean that it abides in the sense of 'repose' which is the opposite of 'motion,' but that it abides in a sense which does not refer either to motion or to rest." Aristotle remarked, with considerable irritation, that Xenophanes "never made anything clear" (οὐδὲν διασαφήνισεν, *Met.*, 986b), and it is quite true that Xenophanes was incapable of employing the dialectical devices which were familiar to Aristotle and to Simplicius; but when these negations are stated in terms of sixth century controversy they become reasonably transparent. Xenophanes denied that Peras (Limit) and the Apeiron were appropriate qualifications of his One God, because both Peras and the Apeiron were regularly employed to explain the processes of physical change, and were actually substantial parts of those processes, and had been identified with Fire or Air or Pneuma or the "opposites" or the changing many. Peras and the Apeiron had been soiled by this contact, and Xenophanes, who had set out to exalt his One God above the processes of physical change, could not possibly apply such terms to the One God. But he could apply them to the phenomena of change; natural processes had sunk in the scale of values and of existence, and had necessarily become mere φαινόμενα (appearances), about which no one could really know anything. The One God, on the contrary, Xenophanes was quite certain about; the One God was pure causality.

For the same reason, Xenophanes rejected the attributes of motion and rest. They are inappropriate, because they suggest the idea of a physical substance that moves or that stops moving and rests; the One God is exalted above physical motion and rest. The One God "abides," but it abides in "the same"; it abides in identity with itself. It is still "coherent with" or "attached to" all things; but it coheres only as a cause coheres with that which is caused. The One God still lives,

but it does not breathe ($\mu\grave{\eta}$ $\mu\acute{\epsilon}\nu\tau\omicron\iota$ $\dot{\alpha}\nu\alpha\pi\nu\epsilon\hat{\iota}\nu$, *FV*, 11 A 1);
it lives the quiet motionless life of eternity instead of the
busy and agitated life of mere immortality. It sees and hears
and thinks, but it does not need the organs of sense or a brain.
The attitude of Xenophanes towards his One God is the attitude of a worshipper who will heap every imaginable perfection upon the object of his worship.

If we contrast Pythagoras with Xenophanes, we can see
the intimate relation between the partial dualism of the one
and the partial monism of the other. Pythagoras worshipped
the One, but was still able to discern, beside the One, enveloped by the One, the changing many; Xenophanes had gazed
so fixedly upon the One God that the changing many had
faded into a world of mere phenomena, a fleeting appearance
of birth and becoming, beside the dazzling vision of the Un-
born and Eternal Cause. "Opinion is upon all things"; and
the scorn with which Xenophanes looks upon all changing
things is the exact counterpart of his worship of the One God.
For the first time in the history of Greek thought, the rational
investigation of nature is explicitly separated from the pursuit of knowledge and wisdom. Pythagoras had prepared the
way, by subordinating the pursuit of knowledge and wisdom
to his desire for salvation and for reunion with the One Fire;
but now Xenophanes has put the aspirations of philosophy
and theology, their quest for truth, on one side of a dividing
line, and has assigned the One God as the object of their
quest. On the other side of the line he has left the changing
many; and that which anyone thinks about the changing many
is neither philosophy nor science, but is mere opinion.

A detailed study of the opinions of Xenophanes would be
irrelevant to our subject, but a glance at them will show his
contempt for the "scientific" ideas current in his time. Men,
and even the psychai of men, consist of earth and water, and
not of the nobler substances air and fire; sun, moon, and stars
are not gods, but luminous clouds or sparks "collected from
the moist exhalation" (*FV*, 11 A 40); new suns rise every

morning, while the old suns have disappeared in the distance; eclipses occur when a sun falls into a hole; the earth dissolves into the sea, and the sea (as is proved by fossils) again dries into earth; the roots of the earth extend downward to infinity. It is clear that Xenophanes made up his mind to heap ridicule upon the beliefs both of ordinary men and of philosophers, and not only upon their beliefs but upon the things themselves which constitute the changing many. Incidentally, we can now explain one of the fragments (*FV*, 11 B 28): "this upper limit (πεῖρας) of earth is visible here by our feet, and this limit flows (καὶ ῥεῖ) as it approaches." The assertion that a limit "flows" seemed unintelligible, and the passage has been rewritten by Diels and Karsten to read "this limit is seen to draw near to air" or "is seen to draw near to aither."[1] But it is obvious that Xenophanes was merely expressing his scorn of "limits" which he believed were subject to constant change and therefore did not really limit or determine; earth, he said, was always changing into water, and therefore the upper limit of earth is *flowing*,[2] instead of remaining fixed as a genuine limit ought.

From this point of view, we may be able to see what becomes of the many gods in the mind of a man who has just proclaimed the One God. The many gods became appearances; they sank in the scale of reality, but they did not cease to exist, any more than phenomena in general ceased to exist. Therefore Xenophanes was not tempted to deny their existence, and he probably explained them all as phenomena of nature; the only definite positive statement we have is that Iris was a cloud (*FV*, 11 B 32). But when Xenophanes had explained the gods as phenomena of nature, he still found himself confronted by the popular stories about anthropomorphic gods, which shocked him just as they had shocked Pythagoras. He could neither deny the plural phenomenal gods nor permit any evil or imper-

---

[1] Diels proposed ἠέρι; Karsten, αἰθέρι. All the MSS. have καὶ ῥεῖ. The text is completely intelligible without alteration.

[2] The limit might almost be said to "fluctuate."

fection to be attributed to them; and he tried to escape from this awkward position by taking refuge in a series of negations. The gods are not immoral; the gods are not begotten; the gods do not die; the gods do not resemble man; the stories of the poets are false; and, most illuminating of all these negations, the truth about the gods can never be exactly known. Since the gods are phenomena, Xenophanes can excuse himself from defining them in terms of reality; but since some phenomena are gods, he will not suffer these privileged phenomena to be defiled by any erroneous opinion.

But Xenophanes was not yet out of trouble. He could assert that the gods did not lie or steal, without involving himself in a discussion of the character of his One God; freedom from sin applied equally to the One God and to the many gods. But Zeus had been represented by the poets as an arrogant and tyrannical master, before whose wrath the other gods exhibited disgusting cowardice; Xenophanes was quite naturally in revolt against such a portrayal of divinity, and indulged in one more negation: "among the gods there is no overlordship; for it is not sanctioned by divine law (ὅσιον) that any god have a master over him: and none of the gods lacks anything at all: and the gods see and hear as wholes and not in parts of them" (*FV*, 11 A 32). What Xenophanes meant is clear enough; he denied that any god could be subject to an arbitrary master, because it was impious to attribute so low a status to any god. This negation was intended to be perfectly consistent with his other doctrine that the One God is greatest among gods and men; the One God is the supremely real cause, and cannot be imagined as behaving arbitrarily or like the human master who lords it over his slaves. The relation between the One God and the many gods is on an entirely different plane, from which these anthropomorphic elements have been eliminated; the One God is supreme as a cause is supreme, and Xenophanes did not foresee that his affirmation of the One God would be taken from its context and set beside his denial that a god may have an anthropomorphic master. Out of their context, the two doctrines create an illusion of inconsistency; and there has been a long debate as to whether Xenophanes was a monotheist, a henotheist, or a polytheist. Xenophanes would probably have been horrified by any one of these appellations, if he could have been brought to understand them; but when his two doctrines are replaced in their context, it is clear that they belong on different levels. The One God belongs to the higher level of truth and reality; and the masterless many gods belong to the lower level of opinion and phenomena.

Xenophanes had opposed the real and immutable One God to the changing unreal. The supreme god of the Ionians had made the concession to appearances of changing its outer aspect and its density; the power and charm of this novel and bold denial of appearances set in motion an unending train of philosophical and theological consequences. Xenophanes intended to glorify the supreme god by removing from it all unworthy attributes; and since mutability seemed an unworthy attribute, he had subtracted reality from the world of change. If one took him seriously, science was henceforth impossible except within the realm of mathematics; the natural sciences would become a series of more or less happy guesses. If one took him seriously, truth was henceforth reserved for the students of philosophy, which had closely resembled and now became identical with theology and with metaphysics. We need not suppose that his elevation of the One God into the realm of metaphysical reality was any barrier to his influence; the conviction that there is something unreal in things that change has played a great part in the history of thought and of philosophy. Common sense has always been inclined to agree with Xenophanes in one very important respect: it has been inclined to regard with disfavor anything that is constantly changing. Change makes common sense uncomfortable; if things keep changing they are difficult to deal with and to master and to understand. This prejudice of common sense played into the hands of Xenophanes; and the principal concession that most subsequent philosophers felt compelled to make to appearances was to offer some explanation of the tie between unchanging reality and a world of changing phenomena.

In still another field the doctrines of Xenophanes produced consequences which far outran his intention. By his assault upon the anthropomorphic gods, he joined with Pythagoras in popularizing allegorical interpretations; and from Theagenes of Rhegium (late sixth century) on, the ingenious stupidity of this device commended it to Greeks of a philosophical bent. Theagenes defended the apparently shocking battle of the gods in *Iliad*, XX, as a mere conflict between natural phenomena: "for they say that Dry fights Wet, Hot Cold, Light Heavy, and Water fights Fire" (*FV*, 72). Anaxagoras, Metrodorus of Lampsacus, Diogenes of Apollonia and Democritus all contributed to the craze; the Stoics devoted to it a large part of their energies, and smoothed the way for the expansive allegorical discourses of Philo and of the Christian Fathers.

In connection with the assault that Xenophanes made upon anthropomorphic gods, we should remember that he denied the possibility of divination. Very few later philosophers agreed with him; and henceforth some theory of divination became a part of nearly all philosophical systems.

CHAPTER VIII

HERACLITUS

HERACLITUS of Ephesus, the greatest of the Ionian philosophers, is said to have flourished at the very end of the sixth century B.C. He fought desperately to save the Ionian supreme god from the attack of Xenophanes; but it was far from easy to combine the Ionian mutable Infinite and Indeterminate Air with the immutable and eternal pure Thought and Causality which was the One God of Xenophanes, and the effort to unite these disparate conceptions of god gave a sharp paradoxical turn to his thought concerning the supreme god and the universe. He was quite conscious of the effort he had made, and he expressed his belief that he had been completely successful in the famous aphorism: "The learning of many things teacheth not understanding, else it would have taught Hesiod and Pythagoras, and again Xenophanes and Hecataeus" (*FV*, 12 B 40). He gives this definition of philosophy: "This one thing is wisdom, to understand Thought (γνώμη), which steers all things everywhere" (Diogenes Laertius, IX, 1).

Diogenes Laertius gives us the best summary of the doctrines of Heraclitus (IX, 7-11):

"All things are composed of Fire and dissolve into Fire; all things come to be in accordance with Destiny and all that exists is bound together by that which runs in opposite directions; and all things are full of Psychai and daimons. . . . The Sun is of exactly the size that it appears to be. . . . You cannot discover the limits of Psyche (Life) though you journey over every way: so deep is its cause [or 'reason': the Greek is λόγος]. He used to call opinion epilepsy, and said that the sense of sight lies. . . .

"Fire is the element, and all things are a gift given in return for Fire, and come into being by rarefaction and condensation. But he gives no clear explanation. All things come into being along opposite ways, and the sum of things flows like a river. The all is limited and the universe is One; the universe is begotten from Fire and again turns into Fire in alternating cycles through all eternity; and this takes place in accordance with Destiny. Of the opposites, the one which leads towards birth is called war and strife, and the one which leads towards the dissolution of all things into Fire is called agreement and peace; and change is the Way Up and Down, and the universe comes into being along this Way. For Fire, when it becomes dense, becomes moisture, and this settles together and becomes water, and water becomes fixed and turns into earth; this process he calls the Way Down. And in its turn again earth is liquified and from it water comes into being, and from this everything else; since Heraclitus refers nearly all upward changes to the Exhalation which comes from the sea; this process he calls the Way Up. Exhalations ($\dot{a}\nu a\theta\nu\mu\iota\dot{a}\sigma\epsilon\iota\varsigma$) come into being from both earth and sea; those from sea are bright and pure, and those from earth dark. He does not make clear the nature of that which surrounds the universe; however he says that there are in it bowls, with the hollow side turned toward us, in which the bright Exhalations collect and produce flames, which are the Stars. . . . The moon, being nearer to the earth, does not move through the pure region: the Sun however moves through a gleaming and unmixed region and keeps a proportionate distance from us. . . . Day and night, months, seasons and years, rains and winds are accounted for by the various Exhalations."

Some of the more important fragments follow:[1]

(1) It is wise to hear not me but the Ordinance,[2] and to agree that the One knows[2] all things.

---

[1] The fragments are here quoted from the excellent edition of Bywater, with his numbering: the arrangement made by Bywater is far superior to that of Diels.

[2] Most editors have adopted λόγου (Reason), the conjecture of Bernays. All the

(2) Men show themselves incapable of understanding the Reason that binds[3] both before they have heard of it and when they hear of it for the first time. For though all things come to be in accordance with this Reason, men appear wholly ignorant, when they make trial of words and deeds such as I describe, dividing each thing according to its nature and explaining how it truly is. But other men do not know what they do when they are awake, just as they forget what they do when they are asleep.

(4) Eyes and ears are bad witnesses to men whose Psychai speak another and an alien language.

(10) Nature loves to hide.

(11) The lord to whom the oracle at Delphi belongs neither speaks out nor hides his meaning, but shows it by a sign.

(17) Pythagoras, son of Mnesarchus, worked out his inquiry more elaborately than any other man, and having made a selection of these writings composed a wisdom of his own, which contains much learning but is fraudulent.

(20) No one of gods or men made this Cosmos, which is the same for all things, but it always was and is and shall be Fire ever-living, kindling in measures and extinguishing itself in measures.

(21) The transformations of Fire are first sea; and half of the sea is earth, and the other half is the Lightning-storm (πρηστήρ).

(22) All things are given in exchange for Fire, and Fire in exchange for all things, as wares are given for gold and gold for wares.

(24) Fire is Want (χρησμοσύνη) and Satiety (κόρος).

(25) Fire lives the death of earth, and air lives the death

MSS. read δόγματος, which is quite intelligible in the sense of Ordinance or Decree, the Law of God: and it seems better to follow the MSS. So all the MSS. read εἰδέναι, "knows"; which I have accordingly translated instead of the conjecture εἶναι, "is."

[3] All the MSS. read τοῦ δέοντος, and since this refers to the function of Reason as the cause of Harmonia, there is no excuse for emendation.

of Fire; water lives the death of air, and earth lives the death of water.

(26) Fire in its advance will judge and condemn all things.

(28) The Lightning steers all things.

(29) The sun will not overstep his measures; if he should, the Erinyes, the allies of Justice, will discover him.

(32) There is a new sun every day.

(36) God is day and night, winter and summer, war and peace, satiety and famine; but he appears different, just as when he mingles with different sorts of incense[4] he is given a name according to each man's fancy.

(41) You could not step twice into the same rivers; for different waters are always flowing along.

(43) Homer was wrong in saying "May strife perish from among gods and men!": because all things would pass away.[5]

(44) War is father of all things and king of all things; and some he has made gods and some he has made men; some he has made slaves and some free men.

(45) They do not understand how that which is at variance agrees with itself; for it is a Harmonia [binding][6] of opposite tensions, as of the bow and of the lyre.

(46) That which opposes is that which unites, and the most beautiful Harmonia is that of opposites.

(47) The invisible Harmonia is mightier than the visible.

(57) Good and evil are the same thing.

(59) Fastenings are things whole and things not whole, that which is drawn together and that which is drawn apart, the

---

[4] The divine Fire "mingles" with different sorts of incense, and burns the incense, and so produces different odors. There is no need to emend by adding θύωμα (incense) with Bernays, or ἀήρ (air) with Zeller.

[5] *Iliad*, XVIII, 107. Burnet was undoubtedly right in adding οἰχήσεσθαι γὰρ πάντα from Simplicius *in Cat.*, 412, 26. Simplicius also explains: "for if one of two opposites fail, all will be destroyed and will vanish."

[6] "Attunement" (Burnet) is scarcely possible. The two readings, παλίντονος (Plutarch) and παλίντροπος (Hippolytus) are equally good: the Binding that "turns back upon itself" is practically equivalent to the Binding "of opposite tensions." In either case, it is the string of the bow and the strings of the lyre that bind: the idea is clearly expressed in 46 and 59.

harmonious[7] and the discordant: the One is made of all things, and all things of the One.

(61) To God all things are beautiful and good and just, but men have supposed that some things are unjust and others just.

(65) The Wise is one only; it is unwilling and willing to be called Zeus.

(68) To Psychai (Lives) it is death to become water; to water it is death to become earth; and water comes into being from earth, and Psyche (Life) from water.

(69) The Way Up and the Way Down is one and the same.

(72) It is a delight to Psychai to become moist.

(76) The dry Light of the sun is the wisest and best Psyche.[8]

(85) Dead bodies are more fit to be cast out than dung.

(91) Thought is common to all. Those who speak with understanding must derive their strength from that which is common to all, as a city-state derives its strength from law in even greater degree. For all human laws are fed by the one Law which is divine. For the divine Law extends its power as far as it pleases, and suffices for all things, and survives all things.

(92) Although Reason is common, the many live as if they had a wisdom of their own.

(95) To those who are awake there is one common cosmos, but those who are asleep turn away each into a cosmos of his own.

(125) The mysteries practised among men are impious mysteries.

(126) And they pray to these images, just as if one were to gossip with houses, not knowing how to recognize gods or heroes.

(130) They try to purify themselves with blood, being mad, just as if one who had stepped into mud tried to wash himself with mud.

---

[7] Here "harmonious" is correct, because the Greek is συνᾷδον, "singing together."
[8] Diels now rejects (FV, 12 B 118) the conjectures of Stephanus, which were adopted by Bywater and by Burnet, and reads αὐγή ξηρή as above.

In addition to these fragments, a most important document on the relation of the human Psyche to Pneuma is furnished by Sextus Empiricus (VII, 127):

"That which contains us is endowed with reason (logos) and with intelligence. According to Heraclitus, this divine Reason we draw in when we breathe, and become endowed with mind; and when we sleep we are forgetful, but on waking are again rational. For during sleep, since the passages of the senses are closed, the mind in us is separated from its union with that which contains us; and only a point of attachment, due to breathing, is preserved as a sort of root. When our mind is thus set apart, it loses the power of memory that it previously possessed; but upon waking it leans outward once more through the passages of the senses as if through windows, and when it has combined with that which contains us it puts on the power of reason. Therefore, just as coals when brought near the fire change and become fiery throughout, but are extinguished when they are separated from it, so the portion which is derived from that which surrounds us, and which as a stranger has received the hospitality of our bodies, becomes almost devoid of reason during this separation, but during its contact through the greatest possible number of passages it is restored in its likeness to the whole. Heraclitus asserts that this common and divine Reason, by partaking in which we become endowed with Reason, is the criterion of truth."

Perhaps the most striking feature of the thought of Heraclitus is the multitude of different titles that he bestows upon the supreme god. Each title corresponds to a different aspect of the divinity that makes all things one. The supreme god is Fire, the One, Psyche (Life and Soul), "that which contains" (τὸ περιέχον) Anathymiasis (Upward Exhalation), Synapsis (Fastening), Harmonia (Binding of opposites), the Way Up and Down, the common Logos (Reason), the one Nomos (Law), Destiny, Lightning, God. To what shall we attribute this vast syncretism?

Heraclitus indulged in bitter language about the lack of understanding of Homer and Hesiod, Pythagoras and Xenophanes, but he was certainly not too proud to learn from his opponents. Pythagoras would have agreed with him in saying that the supreme god is the One, Fire, Psyche, Harmonia, Reason; Xenophanes would have agreed with him in saying that the supreme god is the One, knows all things, and is Reason and Destiny; Anaximenes would have agreed with him in saying that the supreme god is Fire (because divine Fire is merely thinner Air or Pneuma), Psyche, "that which contains us," and the One source of all things through the processes of rarefaction and condensation. If a philosophy could be explained merely by analysing it into a number of component parts, and its parts upon being reassembled would reproduce the living originality of the whole, we should have to confess that the originality of the thought of Heraclitus was much like that of the jackdaw in his borrowed feathers. And it is quite true that Heraclitus had a profound respect for and sympathy with the tradition of Greek thought about the supreme god, and that despite his contempt for his predecessors he did not hesitate to adopt from them and to apply to his own supreme god most of the attributes in which they had expressed their vision of that god. In fact, it was really his respect for the tradition of Greek thought that drove him to make a new and personal synthesis.

Pythagoras had gone far on the path which separated the One Fire from the many, and Xenophanes had achieved the separation of the One God from the living stuff of the universe; nothing was now left to bind the supreme god to the universe except the bond of causation. Against this separation of the supreme god from the changing many and from the living stuff of the universe, Heraclitus reaffirmed the identity of the supreme god with the changing many and with living stuff. Against Pythagoras, he argued that the One Fire was itself all the changing opposites and was not merely present, in some mysterious fashion, in all things, but itself was all things; against Xenophanes, he argued that the One God was not immutable but was the very essence of change, and was not outside the stuff of life but was earth and water and Air and Fire. But when Heraclitus had made this defence of traditional beliefs, his difficulties were by no means over. He was thoroughly aware that Pythagoras and Xenophanes had criticized the tradition about the supreme god in the name of the supreme god's greater perfection. If Heraclitus omitted any attribute of the supreme god which added to that god's perfection, no matter how inconsistent it might seem with the traditional qualities of Fire, the god of Heraclitus would be a failure. Therefore Heraclitus accumulated the names of all the excellent attributes which had been bestowed upon the supreme god by Pythagoras and by Xenophanes, and applied them to his own god; and therefore Heraclitus struggled to demonstrate that his own god both changed and did not change, and was all things and yet was pure causality free from the imperfections of body. The intellectual devices by which he achieved the impossible, to his own satisfaction, deserve our especial scrutiny, because they are the counterpart of the doctrines of Xenophanes: they elevate the Fire of Heraclitus out of the realm of time and change and body into eternity and changelessness.

Heraclitus shared the contempt that Xenophanes felt for the details of physical change, which make up science, and for our eyes and ears, the lying instruments of perception upon which scientists depend. Therefore Heraclitus trusted in Reason, and gave but a brief account of the process of change which forms the universe. His supreme god sets out upon his career as pure Fire, but this Fire already contains within itself two opposites, the one which leads towards birth (known as War and Strife) and the one which leads towards the dissolution of all things into Fire (known as Agreement and Peace); because Fire is thus double, it is a Harmonia or a Fastening of opposites. Harmonia acquires a new meaning; it is no longer first of all the binding action of the One which produces order in the many, but the binding of apparent opposites into a real one. War goes to work; Fire becomes sea; half of the sea becomes earth, and half the Storm of Lightning. The Way Down is completed when earth is formed; and earth is lowest in the scale of values. But earth is constantly dissolving into water, and meantime the rest of the universe is being formed from water. The moment earth begins to dissolve, the Way Up has begun, and the agent which will ultimately dissolve all things into Fire is operating. This agent is the upward Exhalation (Anathymiasis), and is itself double (one from earth, and one from sea). These Exhalations are of course the Heraclitean equivalent of Pneuma; they are fiery and active and rarefying, and in the course of time they convert all into Fire. Besides being Pneuma, they are Psyche, the Breath of Life; "Heraclitus also says that the First Cause is Psyche, or the upward Exhalation out of which he produces all other things; and that Psyche is the least corporeal of things, and is always flowing." This is the testimony of Aristotle (*De Anima*, 405 a), and it is confirmed by the commentaries of Philoponus and Themistius. This Psyche which has no limits is of course the Mind and Soul of the universe; and only by contact with it are our minds kindled into reason.

In this setting, how could Fire change and be immutable, be pure causality and not be an impure body? One of the most important doctrines of Heraclitus was designed to solve the first difficulty, and to contribute to the solution of the second; it might be called the doctrine of Identity by repetition. "The universe is begotten from Fire and again turns into Fire in alternating cycles through all eternity; and this takes place in accordance with Destiny." Anaximander had already taught that infinite universes are born and perish again in infinite succession; and Anaximenes seems to have agreed with his master. Heraclitus seized upon the hint given by his predecessors, and altered the whole meaning of the doctrine by fixing the intervals (κατά τινας περιόδους) at which divine Fire should recapture its perfect unity. He calculated the length of one interval as 10,800 years, and this interval was called the Great Year, since Heraclitus reckoned a generation as thirty years, and 360 × 30 = 10,800. During the Great Year, change is continuous, and Fire exerts all its creative powers; and yet the changes are all "judged and condemned" by the advance of eternal Fire. Fire blots them out, and at the end of every period it is revealed that all those changes were essentially an illusion, and nothing is left of them but Fire. As identity attained by repetition converts change into an illusion, and preserves for Heraclitus and his followers the immutability of the supreme god, so it performs the same operation upon time; the endless torrent of time is arrested, and disappears into the sands of eternity. And yet it has been the fate of Heraclitus, who invented this almost magical artifice for the abolition of real time and real change, to be abused and admired as the philosopher of the "flux." Heraclitus invented the doctrine of the flux, that πάντα ῥεῖ, for a different but wholly consistent purpose, as we have already seen; it was intended to reunite the supreme god with the changing world, from which Xenophanes had separated his One God.

The doctrine of Recurrent Fire also contributed to solve the problem of causality and impure body. If at regular intervals nothing remained except pure Fire, the most subtle and causal of all substances, it seemed to Heraclitus that he had released the supreme god from the impurity and the passivity of body. Therefore Heraclitus did not hesitate to emphasize the comparative baseness of earth and water. He referred to the Path on which they were formed as the Path Down, and as Deficiency or Want (χρησμοσύνη); Psychai die when they become water, and mud is even worse than water. A passage in Clement of Alexandria (*Protrept.*, 10, 75) illustrates this depreciation of the lower forms of Fire: "But there are some who, after the manner of worms, wallow in marshes and mud, which are the streams of pleasure, and feed on profitless and senseless delights; these are swinish men, for swine, says one [Heraclitus], 'take pleasure in mud' more than in pure water." In similar fashion, Heraclitus proclaimed his contempt for dead bodies (Frag. 85). Without the help of his doctrine of Recurrent Fire, he would have been involved in obvious and serious difficulties. He had said that all things were Fire; and since Fire was perfect, why should not all things be perfect? And it is a fact that Heraclitus seems to have been confronted with that question, and to have answered it with the bold affirmation that all things were perfect—in the sight of God (Frag. 61). For the sight of God was the sight of eternity; and God, at recurrent intervals, was to advance upon and judge and condemn, and at the same time cancel, all temporary imperfections by absorbing them into its one Fire.

The lack of consistency in these doctrines of Heraclitus is due, not to any deficiency in his genius, but to the fact that we are, so to speak, outside them; we can only by an effort catch momentary glimpses of them as they would have appeared to Heraclitus himself, illuminated by his faith, and so disposed as to form an organic and living unity. There are plenty of witnesses, both friends and foes, to the enduring influence of Heraclitus; Parmenides was perhaps his greatest foe, and Zeno, founder of the Stoic school, the greatest of his followers.[9]

The philosophy of Xenophanes had induced Heraclitus to go far on the road that ultimately led to the complete distinction between the Aristotelian God (immaterial Reality) and matter ("material" unreality). The supreme god of Heraclitus was still spoken of as changing, but Fire had assumed the dignity of the cause and the agent of change, and its activity was necessarily contrasted with the passivity of that which it caused. But that which is caused by Fire is the lower forms of Fire; and these lower forms take on a degree of relative passivity and unreality which corresponds to their lowly stations in the temporal universe. They become mere intervals in the one active divine reality of Fire. God is the eternal cause, and all change is temporal. The cosmogenetic gods of earlier Greek tradition were as a rule sluggish beings, whose power was

---

[9] Zeller and Burnet have insisted that Stoic influence has seriously distorted the doctrines of Heraclitus as reported in the sources. Burnet (*op. cit.*, 143) says that "the Stoic theories of the λόγος and the ἐκπύρωσις are constantly ascribed" to Heraclitus: this is really not unnatural, because Heraclitus actually invented these theories. The Stoics expanded them, but did not alter their essence.

eclipsed by that of their descendant gods; but the non-anthropomorphic Fire of Heraclitus is no longer merely at the beginning of the series of changes that constitute the cosmos, but is itself the end of the series. Like Kronos, Fire devours its offspring; but none of the offspring escapes Fire, not even the cosmos. In the system of Anaximander, change had been an injustice; now change has become a kind of inevitable and periodic appearance, and the supreme god has become the cause of that appearance.

CHAPTER IX

PARMENIDES

P ARMENIDES of Elea is said to have been influenced by Xenophanes, and by Ameinias, who was a Pythagorean; he seems to have been a slightly younger contemporary of Heraclitus. In bitter opposition to the Fire of Heraclitus, which was now open to criticism as an inadequate attempt to combine a changing supreme god with changelessness, Parmenides rebuilt the One God of Xenophanes.

Thanks to Simplicius, Proclus and Sextus Empiricus, we have fairly extensive fragments of the poem of Parmenides. Parmenides represented himself as having been borne, by a chariot and horses and under the guidance of the Daughters of the Sun, through the gate between the ways of day and night and into the Light, where he received from a kindly goddess a revelation which included both the "immobile heart of persuasive Truth" and "the opinions of mortals in which there is no true belief."

First he learns that "What Is cannot be cut off from What Is; it neither scatters itself in every direction and way through the cosmos nor does it come together" (*FV*, 18 B 2). "What Is, is, and cannot not be" (*FV*, 18 B 4). "For Thinking and Being are the same thing" (*FV*, 18 B 5).[1] "You must say and think that What Is is; for Being is, and non-being is not. I will hold

---

[1] Zeller and Burnet translate "denn dasselbe kann gedacht werden und sein" ("for it is the same thing that can be thought and can be"). Burnet asserts that νοεῖν cannot be the subject of the sentence, "for a bare infinitive is never so used." Gildersleeve, in his *Syntax of Classical Greek*, I, 132 *ff.*, gives 33 examples, from Homer on, of the infinitive without the article, as the subject. Besides, Parmenides argued not that non-being could not be thought, which would be an absurd argument from his point of view, but that it *must* not, and *ought* not to, be treated as a reality.

you back from this first way of inquiry [about non-being], and also from that way which mortals who know nothing imagine, being two-headed; for helplessness guides the wandering mind in their breasts, and they are carried along, being as blind as they are deaf, seized with stupor, an assembly devoid of judgment, who have fancied that to be and not to be 'are the same and not the same,' and that the path that all things follow 'turns back upon itself' " (FV, 18 B 6). "What Is does not come into being and is imperishable, entire, unique, immovable and without end [in time]; it was not and will not be, since it is now one continuous whole. . . . Nor will the strength of true belief permit anything to come into being beside that Which Is out of that which is not; for this reason Justice does not relax her fetters and permit anything to come into being or to perish, but holds fast. . . . Nor is it divisible, since it is all alike; nor is there anything anywhere stronger which could prevent it from being continuous, nor is it anywhere weaker, but all is full of Being. Therefore it is all continuous. . . . Moreover it is immovable within the limits of mighty bonds, without beginning or end in time . . . , and abiding in absolute identity it lies by itself . . . ; for mighty Necessity holds it in the bonds of Limit, which fences it in round about; therefore it is not in accordance with divine Law [Themis] that What Is be incomplete; for it is not in need of anything, but if it were in need of anything it would need everything.[2] The same is also Thinking [νοεῖν] and the cause of Thought; for without What Is, in which Thinking finds its expression, you cannot discover Thinking; for there is not and never will be anything outside of What Is, since Fate binds it to be entire and immovable. Therefore it has been called all things [given every name] that mortals have set aside for it, believing them to be true names—'coming to be' and 'perishing,' 'being' and 'non-being,' 'change of place'

---

[2] Reading ἐὸν δ' ἂν παντὸς ἐδεῖτο with the MSS. ἐπιδευές must be supplied from the clause preceding. Burnet supplies ἀτελεύτητον, and translates "if it were infinite, it would stand in need of everything": but ἀτελεύτητον does not here mean "infinite," and "in need" is demanded by the syntax and by the thought.

and 'alteration of bright color.' Since then there is an extreme Limit, What Is is complete on every side, like the form of a rounded sphere, of equal strength from the centre in every direction . . . , for there is nothing that could stop it from extending equally, nor is it possible that there be more of What Is in one place and less in another, since it is all Inviolable. Here I close my trustworthy speech and thought about truth; henceforth learn the beliefs of mortals and heed the deceptive order of my verses. Mortals have set aside in their minds two Forms, one of which must not be named, and that is the point in which they have gone astray; they have judged them to be opposites in form, and have assigned to them distinctive characters separating them from each other; to one the aitherial flaming Fire, which is gentle and very light [weightless], and identical with itself throughout; to the other no such qualities, but it is in itself the opposite, night devoid of understanding, a solid and heavy form. This ordering of the universe I tell you of as it seems likely to be in every respect, for so no thought of mortals can surpass you. . . . Now that all things have been named Light and night, and the names have been assigned to this and to that according to the powers of Light and night, all is full at the same time of Light and of invisible night, since neither has anything in common with the other. . . . And you shall know the nature of Aither, and all the signs in the Aither . . . and how the Sky that contains us came to be and how Necessity brought it and bound it to be the Limits of the Stars. . . . In the midst of these [bands of Fire and night] is the divine power that steers all things" (the Pythagorean central Fire, cf. Simplicius *in Phys.*, 34, 12 *ff.*).

The supreme god of Parmenides bears a general resemblance to the One God of Xenophanes; it is the one supreme reality, and all else consists of unreal and changing appearances. Like the One God, the One Being of Parmenides had to be defined mostly in negative terms, because Parmenides was seeking to establish a more nearly perfect definition of the supreme god against what seemed to him the defects of the Heraclitean Fire

and of the Pythagorean One Fire. A great many of these negations apply equally to the doctrines of Heraclitus and to those
of Pythagoras, but it is possible to distinguish a few that have
a special and limited application. For example, Parmenides
prohibits "this first way of inquiry" which teaches that "non-
being is," and couples with it a prohibition of a second way of
inquiry which teaches that "to be and not to be are the same
and not the same," and that "the path that all things follow
turns back upon itself." The reference to Heraclitus as the
"blind and deaf and stupefied" author of the second way is
clear enough; but to whom shall we attribute the first way?
The Ionians are excluded; they believed that Water or the
Apeiron or Air made up the whole sum of reality. Heraclitus
is excluded, because the second way of inquiry belongs to him.
Xenophanes is excluded, because he and Parmenides are in
agreement. No one is left but Pythagoras; and the doctrine that
"non-being is" is the Parmenidean phrase for the partial dualism of Pythagoras, who had taught that the One Fire was a
Harmonia, and that it combined with and lent its own reality
to certain portions of infinite and indeterminate stuff, called
"the other." The extreme politeness with which Parmenides
treats the dualism of Pythagoras is due to the fact that he himself accepts, in the realm of mortal opinion, a supreme god of
Fire which is in many respects analogous to the Pythagorean
One Fire.

The One Being of Parmenides is continuous; it is not scattered and divided as the One Fire was divided. It is eternal,
entire, and immovable, precisely like the One God of Xenophanes; it abides in the "same," precisely like the One God; it
is all Thinking, precisely like the One God; but it is held in the
"bonds of Limit," and in this respect it seems to differ from
the One God. Xenophanes had rejected the attributes Peras
(Limit) and Apeiron (infinite and indeterminate) because they
had been applied to changing things; now Parmenides restores
Peras as an item in the perfection of his One Being, and takes
great pains to make the meaning of the term clear. First he as-

serts that the goddess Justice does not "relax her fetters" and permit anything to come into being or to perish; that is to say, a divine power employs "fetters" ($\pi\epsilon\delta\alpha\iota$) to prevent Being from undergoing change. Next we are told (B 8, v. 26) that Being is immovable "within the Limits of mighty bonds," because coming-to-be and destruction "have wandered far away" from Being; and Being abides in absolute identity and lies by itself and "thus remains forever firm," because the divine power of mighty Necessity "holds it in the bonds of Limit, which fences it in round about." In both these passages Limit is conceived as the equivalent of the fetters of Justice; Limit prevents motion, which here as so often in Greek means "change," and Limit establishes a boundary round Being, beyond which there is change, but within which Limit preserves the immutability of Being.

In the next sentence Parmenides introduces a new negative qualification of Being; "therefore it is not in accordance with divine law that What Is be incomplete ($\dot{\alpha}\tau\epsilon\lambda\epsilon\dot{\upsilon}\tau\eta\tau o\nu$), for it is not in need of anything, but if it were in need of anything, it would need everything." That is to say, the supreme god has Limit and cannot change, and therefore it has attained an End ($\tau\epsilon\lambda\epsilon\upsilon\tau\dot{\eta}$), in the sense that it is complete and finished and perfect; if it were incomplete, unfinished, and imperfect, it would be "in need of something," and would be altogether unsuited to the rôle of a supreme god, or as Parmenides puts it "would need everything." The End that One Being has attained is the achievement of perfection; and the source of its perfection is its immutability. Parmenides continues the argument about Peras in B 8, vv. 42 *ff.*: "Since there is an extreme [$\pi\dot{\upsilon}\mu\alpha\tau o\nu$, uttermost or final] Limit, Being is complete on every side, like the form of a well-rounded sphere, of equal strength from the centre in every direction, for it must not be at all stronger or weaker anywhere; . . . and it is all Inviolable, for since there is equality throughout Being, Being lies uniformly within Limits." This apparently harmless passage contains within it the seeds of much controversy, and therefore requires

[85]

careful analysis. When Parmenides uses the epithet "Inviolable," he is laying stress upon the sanctity of the supreme god, but when he says that the One Being is all Inviolable, and proves this point by affirming the even uniformity of Being, he is undoubtedly arguing against what seems to him an erroneous opinion. The error of his opponent must have consisted in asserting that the supreme god was not uniformly and evenly distributed, and if we put ourselves in the position of hostile critics, we can perceive that such an assertion might be attributed to any predecessor of Parmenides with the one exception of Xenophanes. Against the rarefied and condensed Air of Anaximenes and the Pythagorean One Fire, concentrated at the centre and the circumference of the cosmos and scattered in every microcosm, Parmenides sets up a series of negations; the One Being is not rarefied here and condensed there, or scattered within the cosmos in unequal portions, but is uniform and even, and therefore its sanctity, its holy immutability, is not confined to parts of it but covers it all. The same explanation applies to the assertion that Being is of equal strength from the centre in every direction; Parmenides is denouncing the error of making the supreme god strong in one place and weak in another. But there is a new element in this assertion; it suddenly develops, as we work backward through the passage, that the supreme god has a centre. What can a supreme god, which is all Thought and Being, possibly do with a centre? More especially, what can such a god do with a centre which is a mere imaginary point, and which is not differentiated from the rest of Thought and Being by any qualitative difference whatever, but purely by its position? Furthermore, we discover that the One Being not only has a centre, but resembles the *form* of a rounded sphere, and that it has an extreme Limit which bounds it and "completes" it at every point on the periphery of its spherical form.

Hitherto, Parmenides has used Limit and End to denote a metaphorical boundary between changing phenomena and divine immutability, between non-being and Being. Limit has therefore appeared to us, and has been accepted by our minds, as a purely metaphysical term which makes an intellectual distinction between two concepts; and now Parmenides tells us that this intellectual distinction has, without any warning, become the bounding line or periphery of a sphere which like any other sphere has a centre. We quite naturally feel inclined to accuse Parmenides of an intellectual crime; the first inclination of every reader when he comes upon something hard to understand is to ascribe entire responsibility to the author. However, in this particular case the difficulty in understanding Parmenides is really our fault; when we hear the word "sphere," we allow our minds to go off on a tangent, like unruly dogs who have smelt something more exciting, or more familiar, than the scent they were supposed to follow. A sphere suggests to us something round and solid, like a marble or the earth; and some historians have yielded to the suggestion, and have decided that Parmenides was a "corporeal" monist, and that the sphere he speaks of is full of matter or of body. Now that we are on our guard, we ought to be able to keep our minds on the trail. The sphere of which Parmenides speaks is a sphere full of Thought and Being, and the periphery or Peras of this sphere is a purely intellectual boundary and has nothing material or corporeal about it. We are well aware that there is a kind of sphere that has a purely intellectual boundary or limit; it is the sphere that mathematicians use, and it is a purely intellectual or logical form. What Parmenides has done does not involve, from his po:nt of view, any change in the meaning of Peras; he has merely said that his supreme god is a Form, and that it is a spherical Form. In fact, what we behold in this passage is the birth of the idea that the supreme god is not merely the supreme reality and the supreme causal power, but is also the supreme Form, and we are in attendance, so to speak, at one of the central mysteries of Greek philosophy.[3] How can

[3] It is of course true that Pythagoras knew something about geometry: and it is therefore certain that the idea of causal forms was at least implicit in his system. But we do not know whether he expressly connected his causal numbers with causal forms: it is however probable that he ascribed causal power to some

a form have divine power? And why should the divine Form that Parmenides has brought to birth be any particular form? Why should Being and Thought wear the shape of a sphere and not, for example, of a cube?

The answer to these questions is not far to seek. The One Thought, which is the One Being, has been severed by Parmenides from the world of changing phenomena just as far as he dared, or could, sever the one from the other. The universe that we actually experience is constantly changing; and Parmenides has cut every bond that unites the universe of our experience to the supreme and immutable divine power except one. The one bond that remains is the bond of causality, and Parmenides felt himself compelled to maintain the causal bond between his supreme god and the changing universe. If he had failed to maintain it, he would have destroyed the perfection of his supreme god. From the earliest days of Greek thought, a god had been a power, and the power of every god had been manifested, and at the same time tested, in the only universe that we know anything about. The supreme god of the poets and of the philosophers had always been the supreme cause, and we have followed the process by which the supreme god was step by step, and in the name of its greater perfection, dissociated from that which it caused, the process by which the supreme god tended to become immutable Reality, just as that which it caused tended to become mutable unreality. But there was a point in this "progress," which led apparently upward towards the "realm of Light," where a halt had to be called. What would a supreme god amount to if his "power" were to be exercised over absolutely nothing? What would be the use of a supreme cause that had absolutely no effects? It was all very well for Parmenides to speak of phenomena as "non-being," but if they were really absolute non-being, they would dis-

forms, and among others to the pentagram or pentalpha, which had the function of averting evil daimons and preserving health (cf. Lucian, *pro lapsu, 5*). Pythagoras certainly taught that the form of the universe was a sphere.

appear entirely, and the supreme One Being would disappear along with them into the limbo reserved for causes that have no effects. Therefore Parmenides was forced to argue that Being was after all the cause of something, and was driven to look about for and to discover some aspect of the world of change, some attribute of phenomena, which could be represented as the effect which Being caused, and which at the same time, since every effect is inseparably related to its cause and must in some sense resemble its cause, could also be represented as an attribute of Being without seeming to mar the perfection of Being. And Parmenides believed that the shape of the changing universe was precisely the attribute for which he sought, the one relic of and effect of immutable Being in the world of nonbeing, and the only attribute that Being could share with nonbeing without degradation. Therefore Parmenides said that Being was Form, and that the Form of Being was "like a well-rounded sphere." Therefore the Limit, that bounds this sphere of pure Being, coincides with and is the divine cause of the Limit that bounds the sphere of non-being, and the supreme god of Parmenides is still causally connected with the world of phenomena, and is still present in that world as its total and causative Form.

Henceforth the notion of divine causative Form dominates Greek philosophy and theology, and all Greek thinkers who are curious about the world of phenomena will seek to trace out in it the effects of divine Form, which is also Thought and Being, as those effects are manifested in the production of forms in the world of phenomena. And in this world of phenomena and among the forms that are discoverable in it, the same scale of values that has now been established will endure; the forms that change least will be most nearly like the supreme god, and those that change most will be most imperfect. No science that deals with phenomena can be a real science, since real science, so Parmenides and his followers believe, deals exclusively with the immutable perfection of Thought and Being and Form, and that is the Way of Truth. Nevertheless phenomena and "non-being" do not utterly cease to exist, even for Parmenides; and therefore Parmenides, through the goddess who spoke for him, was compelled to add "the beliefs of mortals" to his "trustworthy speech and thought about Truth." The beliefs of mortals are of course the pseudo-science that deals with phenomena; and this section of the poem of Parmenides finds its exact parallel in the "myths" of Plato, or as Plato himself puts it in the *Timaeus* (29 C): "What Being is to becoming, Truth is to belief." Aristotle makes the same distinction: "As for the formal First Cause, it is the task of First Philosophy to determine whether it is One or Many . . . but as for the forms that occur in nature and are perishable, we shall discuss them in our treatise on physics" (*Phys.*, 192). And Parmenides "believes" the views that he puts forward under the category of beliefs of mortals just as much and just as little as Plato and Aristotle believe in their own systems of physics. His personal pride was involved in his personal version of the beliefs of mortals, and we have all known wise men who defend their opinions on subjects about which they know very little, with quite as much zeal as they exhibit in defending what they believe to be the truth.

The first and most conspicuous difference between the Way of Truth and the way of belief is due to the fact that the way of belief contains two forms, "one of which must not be named." This phrase admirably expresses the reluctance that Parmenides felt when the force of his own argument compelled him to retain, though attenuated and filed down to the verge of breaking, the causal bond of Form ($\mu o \rho \phi \acute{\eta}$). Here in the world of phenomena there must be one more form, which will correspond with the One divine Form as the effect corresponds with its cause. At the boundaries or limits of this second form, its coincidence with the divine causal Form will be perfect, and the form of non-being will therefore be a sphere; Parmenides accordingly says that all "is full at the same time of Light and

PARMENIDES

of night devoid of understanding."[4] But though the two forms coincide at their limits, in every other respect they are opposites, since non-being is the opposite of Being; and Parmenides works out the opposite attributes of Being and of non-being as they appear in the world of phenomena, and goes into considerable detail which is irrelevant to our subject. It should be noted, however, that Parmenides has placed himself in a position where he must attribute to the Form of Being many qualities which it did not possess when it abode alone in the Way of Truth; it is now, so to speak, keeping bad company, which is full of negative attributes such as darkness and lack of understanding and solidity and heaviness, and therefore the supreme god, who when alone was pure Being and Thought and Form, promptly acquires the additional attributes of Aither and Flame and Fire and Light, and is spoken of as being "gentle" and "weightless." These additional attributes are the entrance-fee that the supreme god pays for admission to the world of becoming. It was only right that it should be made to pay a fee, since it had already borrowed from that world its own perfect Form.

If it costs the supreme god something to enter the world of phenomena, it is still more expensive for it to remain enclosed in the metaphysical world of pure Being and Thought and Form. When we remember that the supreme god of the Greeks set out upon its career accompanied by the attributes of Life (Psyche), and that the supreme god was then most intimately associated with all that changes and grows and lives, and that it communicated its own Life to the world, we can see that the metaphysical One Being of Parmenides, in spite of its intellectual splendor, has lost some of the most valuable attributes of the earlier god. With the one exception of the dubious and equivocal concept of Form, which still relates it to the changing universe and casts the shadow of extension upon its meta-

4 Parmenides thus anticipated the Stoic doctrine of κρᾶσις δι' ὅλου (total inter-penetration), which was used by Zeno to express the omnipresence of God in matter.

[91]

physical purity, it is set apart from that which lives. In the quest for perfection, it has exchanged living immortality for immutable eternity: the Greek philosophers who brought about this exchange supposed that the exchange was so much sheer profit. Why should it not be? Had they not followed the argument of human reason "whithersoever it led"? And yet it is clear enough that human reason had led them boldly into a *cul-de-sac*, and that human reason, unless it can dilate itself sufficiently to enable it to deal with what lives and changes, is an arrogant and inadequate guide. From this point of view, the rest of the history of philosophy down to our own time is a record of the attempts made by human reason to combine its involuntary worship of the immutable with a greater degree of attention to the facts of life. Human reason, or intelligence, call it what we will, is probably capable of partial and limited amendment in this direction; but the effort required is great, and the ordinary philosopher or scientist, like the ordinary man in any other field, is inclined to do his thinking in the easiest way.

Zeno of Elea and Melissus of Samos, the two disciples of Parmenides, were in general agreement with their master, and their relation to the Eleatic system may be compared to the relation of Chrysippus to Stoicism. Their only importance for our subject lies in the fact that Zeno by his famous paradoxes "demonstrated" the utter impossibility of the very ideas of the many (pluralism), of space and void, and of motion, and that Melissus carried this dialectical process still further. Melissus found that he could not get rid of the notion of the void, unless he extended Being to infinity, and therefore he departed from orthodoxy in this particular. This notion of infinite Being was taken by Aristotle to refer not to the denial of the void but to the denial of determination; and therefore Aristotle said that "Melissus seems to fasten on that which is one in matter" (*Met.*, 986 b), and denounced Melissus as "a little too countrified." This mistake on the part of Aristotle is only worth mention because it has been taken seriously by some scholars; as a matter of fact, Melissus (*FV*, 20 B 9) maintained zealously the orthodox tenet that Being had no body (σῶμα) or thickness (πάχος).[5] The dialectical orthodoxy of Zeno and Melissus had the usual reward; it assisted in bringing to birth the great Eleatic heresy of Leucippus and Democritus.

[5] The μέγεθος that Melissus attributed to divine Being was not material extension in space, but the infinite "greatness" of Being which prevented it from having limits in time, as Melissus argued in Fragment 4 (*FV*, 20 B) : "nothing that has a beginning and an end is eternal or infinite."

CHAPTER X

EMPEDOCLES AND ANAXAGORAS

E MPEDOCLES (about 483-423 B.C.) of Acragas (Gir-
genti) was the first Greek theologian or philosopher to
divide the supreme god into parts. His purpose was essentially the same as that of Heraclitus, and he replied to Parmenides as Heraclitus had replied to Xenophanes. Scandalized
by the mistakes of his predecessors who had "wandered everywhere" and vainly imagined that they had "found the whole"
though both their senses and their minds had been too feeble
to grasp the truth, Empedocles announced that he was a god,
and that he would reveal as much as "divine Law permitted
creatures of a day to hear" (*FV*, 21 B 2, 4).

There are "four Roots (ῥιζώματα)[1] of all things; gleaming
Zeus, life-bringing Hera, Aidoneus, and Nestis who wets with
her tears the springs of mortals" (6). "Being will always be,
wherever one may keep thrusting it" (12); "there is no void in
the All, nor is there anything excessive" (13). "At one time
Being grows to be One [produced] out of Many; at another,
Being divides to be Many [produced] out of One. There is a
double becoming of perishable things and a double departure
out of Being; one becoming is produced and is destroyed by the
coming together of all things, the other becoming is nurtured
and then flies apart as all things are divided. This process of
change never ceases; now all things assemble into One by the
agency of Love, now they are borne asunder by the enmity that
is Strife. Because the One has learned how to come into being
out of Many, and because the One divides again and forms the
Many, in this respect things come into being and they have no

---

[1] He borrowed this term from Pythagoras.

abiding Life; but because this change never ceases, in this respect they are forever immovable in a circle" (17). The Many here spoken of are six in number: "Fire and Water and Earth and the immense height of Air; and apart from these destructive Strife, in every way a match for them, and Love in the midst of them, their equal in length and breadth" (17). These six gods are all "equal and alike in race, but one rules over one function and another over another, and each has its own character, but they have the mastery in turn as time goes round" (17). These six gods make up all Being, but they "running through one another become different things" (17); "there is no real birth (or growth) of any of all mortal things, nor is there any real fulfilment of destructive death, but there is only mixture and separation" (8). When the six gods are under the dominion of Love, Strife passes out to "the outermost boundaries of the circle," and the "gentle-minded immortal impulse of perfect Love advances to the centre of the whirl," and forms one supreme god, called the Sphairos (Sphere), which is "rendered motionless in the close covering of Harmonia, and rejoices in its circular repose" (35, 27).

In the period in which Love is increasing, previous to the formation of the Sphairos, "heads spring up without necks, and naked arms wander about without any shoulders" (57), and as "one divine power [daimon] mingles more and more with another, these things constantly fall into union, wherever each one happens to meet another" (59). When the Sphairos begins to dissolve, under the growing power of Strife, our own world is formed: at first there was a Golden Age, while Love was still strong, and the people of that time "had no Ares as a god nor Kydoimos, nor King Zeus nor Kronos nor Poseidon, but Kypris [Love][2] was their Queen," and they did not sacrifice any living thing. But now men never cease from murder, and since they eat animals, "a father slaughters his own son, who has changed his form" into that of an animal (136, 137). When a god sins by polluting his hands with blood or by following

[2] Aphrodite.

Strife, "he must stray during thirty thousand seasons [ten thousand years] apart from the Blessed, being born in all sorts of forms of mortals, exchanging one hard way of life for another; for the mighty Aither drives him into the Sea, and the Sea spits him out upon the solid Earth, Earth hurls him into the brilliant light of the Sun, and the Sun flings him into the eddies of Aither." Empedocles himself is such an exile from the gods (115).

All living things draw breath in and breathe out through pores; the "blood round the heart is the thought of men" (105), and "by Earth we see Earth, by Water we see Water, by Aither we see divine Aither, and by Fire destroying Fire, by Love we see Love (στοργή), and Strife by grievous Strife" (109), since "out of these all things are fixed and fitted together, and by these they think and feel pleasure and pain" (107). The eye, for example, is made of "ancient Fire, enclosed within membranes and delicate tissues" (84) by Aphrodite, and has but a small portion of Earth. Blood and the "forms of other flesh" are made of Earth, after "she has anchored in the perfect harbors of Kypris,"[3] Hephaistos (Fire), Water, and Aither, mixed in almost equal proportions (98). The process of incessant change is carried on by effluences (ἀπορροαί); tiny portions of all things are forever leaving them (89).

The supreme god is not anthropomorphic, but "is only a sacred and unutterable Mind (φρήν), which darts through the whole cosmos with swift thoughts" (134); and "the Law of all things is extended everywhere, through the wide-ruling Aither and the infinite Light" (135). The Sphairos or supreme god is most perfect when it is completely integrated under the influence of Love, and during the cosmic period in which the power of Love is growing, there is a good deal of free play in nature (τύχη); "many creatures with double faces and double breasts were born," and men "with the heads of oxen," and androgynes (61). Those combinations survived of which the parts were able to render mutual aid (Simplicius, *Phys.*, 371, 4); and

---

[3] The metaphor is Pythagorean: cf. the Hull and the Keel of the universe.

Love is uniformly represented as a divine power that makes for perfection. Strife on the contrary makes for imperfection, and at last disintegrates the perfect One into the Many, in which the five gods Fire, Air, Water, Earth and Love are completely separated from one another. During the cosmic period in which the power of Strife is growing, there is a good deal of Necessity in nature. Every Psyche or Soul is a subordinate divine power; and if it has ever put its trust in Strife, it is separated, by the divine ordinance of Necessity, from the company of the blessed long-lived gods, and is punished by being driven along the circle of birth in this world of disintegration and mortality. Psychai that are wise and abstain from evil are rewarded; "at last they appear among men on earth as diviners, song-writers, physicians and leaders, and from this condition they are born again as gods exalted in honors, sharing the hearth and the table of the other immortal gods, and are free from the griefs of men" (146, 147). Even in this world, the wise Soul has immense privileges. "If you will support yourself on your firm mind and study these things with good disposition and pure contemplation, you shall have all these things in abundance throughout life, and you will gain from them many others. . . . But if you long for other things, such as the countless evils that blunt the thoughts of men, these [good] things will soon desert you as time goes round, since they long to return to their own kind; for know that all things have intelligence and a share of thought. And you shall learn of all drugs that are a defence against sickness and old age, since for you alone will I accomplish all this. You shall arrest the violence of unwearying winds that sweep against the earth and waste the fields; and again if you so please you shall bring back their blasts. You shall cause for men a seasonable drought after dark rain, and cause after summer drought streams that pour down from the Aither to feed the trees. You shall bring out of the house of Hades the strength of a man that has perished" (110, 111).

The theology of Empedocles is indissolubly united to his

philosophy, and is in fact indistinguishable from it. His theology is animated throughout by the same purpose that animated Heraclitus; he has resolved to plunge the One God back into the world of change, because he is unsatisfied by the shadowy Parmenidean bond of Form and believes that divine power is genuinely present in this world, because he believes that Life (Psyche) and change, good and evil, are in some sense realities and not mere phenomena, and because he is at heart, though not in mathematical prowess, a Pythagorean. And yet he is confronted by, and partially believes in, the Eleatic doctrine which maintains that the supreme god, in order to be perfect, must be changeless. The difficulty is obvious, and he overcame it to his own satisfaction by a series of doctrines which are the intellectual equivalent of the Heraclitean doctrines of Recurrent Fire, of the Way Up and the Way Down, and of the lower forms of Fire.

The Sphairos, which is the supreme One God, comes back to identity with itself at fixed periods under the agency of the divine power of Love; and all the combinations and separations that take place in the substance of the One God, though they are in some degree real, are not absolutely real, but are cancelled into perfection by the victory of Love. This is the tribute that Empedocles pays to the perfect Being of Parmenides. But the process of change is also a reality; and therefore the Sphairos changes gradually into the Many Gods, and during this change Love and Strife, Zeus, Hera, Aidoneus and Nestis are manifested as the six different divine realities that have the divine power of accounting for all change. This is the tribute that Empedocles pays to facts. The causal power of Strife is equivalent to the Way Down of Heraclitus, and we remember that the Way Down also had the name of War (Polemos). The causal power of Love is equivalent to the Way Up, which also had the name of Peace. Heraclitus apparently thought of Fire as a traveller who voluntarily took the Way Down; Empedocles has altered the metaphor, and represents his supreme god as yielding to the claims of Strife, which are presented "in the fulness of time" and are sanctioned by a sacred Oath (30). Fire on the journey passed through its own lower forms; but Empedocles has given to Earth, Water and Air a separate and real existence, as well as to Fire. Fire has ceased to "travel" and to change, except in so far as rearrangement is change; therefore in the system of Empedocles there are no lower forms of Fire; and Earth, Water and Air become divine powers coordinate with Fire. These four "elemental" gods are alive throughout (110), and they account for all the changes that take place in the universe and are the complete equivalent of the sum total of divine power in the Sphairos, with one very important exception. They cannot account for change unless they are constantly rearranged; and the remainder of the divine power of the Sphairos is represented as the two gods, Love and Strife, that cause the rearrangement. The power of these two gods must be exercised in gradual alternation; the power of the one grows in exact proportion as the power of the other diminishes, and the temporary victory of one means the temporary defeat of the other. But Love is good and brings about divine Unity in the Sphairos, while Strife is evil and brings about divine diversity in the Many. Therefore good and evil are realities, and life has a meaning even for the mortal men who are, after all, the evanescent product of the immortal gods (36). Wisdom, which guarantees the purification of the Psyche and its harmony with Love, can accomplish apparent miracles; it can even reunite the Psyche, the Life and Soul of a man, with the blessed gods. And though the blessed gods are not strictly immortal, with the exception of the six highest gods, they are "long-lived," and they abandon their lives of separation only to be merged in the perfect immortality of the Sphairos.

A good deal has been said, by those who imagine that Greek philosophy is primarily scientific, about the contributions that Empedocles made to science. It is quite true that Empedocles had great influence on the medical school of Philistion, that he had vague but interesting notions of organic adaptation and evolution, that he invented a theory of perception, and that he proved the reality of Aither (Air) by an experiment with the clepsydra (water-clock). From the point of view of an historian of science, these ideas are undoubtedly contributions to science. But if we are to judge Empedocles rightly, we must bear in mind his own point of view, from which "scientific" theories about events in nature were primarily contributions to theology, to knowledge of the Sphairos and of the six great gods which were its equivalent. Empedocles did not intend, by his experiment with the clepsydra, to prove that "air is a thing"; he intended to prove that divine Aither was a reality, and that the Pythagorean notion of the void was false. In like manner, his theory of perception was designed to show how the god within (Fire, Air, Earth, or Water) can meet and know the same god outside the percipient; and his theory of effluences was in perfect accord with the theological doctrine that Love and Strife were constantly combining and separating small portions of the other four gods.

When we turn to the main features of the theology of Empedocles, and compare his system with those of his predecessors, we can distinguish at least two startling innovations. For the first time in the history of Greek thought, two distinct classes of ultimate divine reality have been established.[4] Love and Strife are just as real as the other four great gods, but they are endowed with a specialized causal function, and are peculiarly responsible for the periodic combination and separation of the other four gods. It has been said that Love and Strife are corporeal, and it is quite true that they alternately extend and contract; but their extension is not that of a body, but that of a cause which is represented as coextensive with the field of its activity. Furthermore, the contrast between the two causes and the four gods which are their field of activity is not such a contrast as we should expect. We habitually think of a cause of motion as active, and of that which is made to move as passive. But Empedocles has invented what appears to be a new and

---

[4] The partially dualistic systems of Pythagoras and of Parmenides contain only one class of ultimate divine reality, the One Fire and the One Being.

strange relation between these two classes of divine reality; Love and Strife are active, but the other four gods, on which they operate, are not passive, are not inert or material elements in any ordinary sense of those terms, but are living and causal divine "substances." The causal power of Love, instead of being "mechanical," as is often said, resembles the "influence" that one living being exerts upon another living being; Love is the cause of mutual and active desire, and creates in Zeus, Hera, Nestis and Aidoneus a longing for the perfect Unity that they attain in the Sphairos. What then is meant by the use of such a term as "mixture," when Empedocles says that "there is no growth or death of any mortal thing, but only mixture and separation"? If we remember that Empedocles is speaking of "mortal things," his meaning becomes quite clear; what we call the birth and death of mortal beings is really the mixture and separation of immortal Beings, and might with no loss of precision be designated by the unmechanical terms of marriage and divorce.

The causal power of Strife presents us with a new problem, and with the second startling innovation for which Empedocles is responsible. For the first time, a full-grown and definite Devil appears on the stage of Greek thought. It is only fitting that Empedocles, who believed himself to be a fallen god, should have had the privilege of introducing the divine reality that had caused his own fall. This is not the place to go into the history of the Devil, although the inquiry is fascinating. From the time of Homer on, the protests of both poets and philosophers against the association of the supreme god with evil had been loud and continuous. In Dionysiac and Orphic legend, the Titans were divine powers of evil, but their power had scarcely survived their destruction by Zeus except in the enfeebled form of mankind, sprung from their ashes. Greek philosophers had hitherto failed to deal explicitly with the principle of evil; they had confined themselves to the task of so defining the supreme god that it should be free from the shadow of evil. But the supreme god was the supreme reality, and change if not a positive evil was at least regarded as an imperfection. Hence "otherness," the diversity of that which changes, had come to be equivalent to a kind of negative and unreal evil; diversity was not a genuine principle of evil merely because diversity had no real being. This was the situation when Empedocles set about his task of reinstating the supreme god in a world in which diversity was no longer a deceiving phenomenon but a fact; and since Strife brought about the complete separation of Love and of the other four great gods, and was the source of that mode of Being in which it was furthest from the perfection of the Sphairos, Strife is a causal power that can fairly be identified with the Devil. Not all changes are evil; only those that are brought about, or rather encouraged, by Strife are evil. The four gods have a native tendency each to rejoin scattered portions of its own Being, and that native tendency is reinforced by Strife. Strife leads the universe on the Way Down, and leads the Psychai of all living beings along the circle of birth through ten thousand years of suffering and death; and only philosophy, as it has been revealed to the god Empedocles, can mitigate human suffering and restore the Soul to union with the blessed gods, along with whom it will ultimately be absorbed into the perfect life of the Sphairos.

Such was the philosophy of Empedocles. It has been said that "it was too passionate to be really systematic"; on the contrary, it would be more just to say that it was the passion of Empedocles, his longing for a religious and philosophical doctrine of the supreme god that would permit the salvation of man, which drove him to expand his original intuition into a system. If we are willing to follow the direction of his thought, the individual dogmas will be seen as the parts of an organic whole. But if we are more attracted by modern science than by the religious fervor of Empedocles, the sap of life that connects his dogmas one with another will cease to flow, and his ideas, that were held aloft in the atmosphere of living divinity, will flutter to the ground; Zeus and Nestis, Hera and Aidoneus, will seem to wither into mere elements, and Love and Strife will be transformed into mere mechanical motive forces.

Anaxagoras (about 500-428 B.C.) of Clazomenae in Asia Minor journeyed to Athens when he was about forty, and lived there until a few years before his death. While in Athens, he became the friend and teacher of Pericles, and he was finally driven back to Clazomenae as the result of his condemnation for impiety in a suit brought by the enemies of Pericles. He was charged with teaching that the sun was a red-hot stone and that the moon was made of earth; the pious and popular view was that all the heavenly bodies were gods, and the popular view was supported by nearly all the philosophers.

The principal fragments are as follows:[5]

(1) All things were together, infinite both in number [or quantity] and in smallness; [this was so] because the small was infinite. And when all things were together, nothing could be seen, because of the smallness of everything; for Air and Aither held all things strongly, being both of them infinite; for among all things taken together Air and Aither are the greatest both in quantity and in magnitude.

(2) For Air and Aither separate themselves [or are separated] from the greatest part of that which surrounds the universe; and that which surrounds is infinite in quantity.

(3) For there is no smallest of that which is small, but there is always a smaller; for Being cannot be non-being. And there is always a greater of that which is great. And the quantity of the great is equal to the quantity of the small; and each thing by itself is both great and small.[6]

(4) Since these things are so, we must think that there are many things and things of every sort in all the universes that are being combined, and that there are in them Seeds of all things, and that these Seeds have every sort of form and color and sensible quality. And human beings are put together, and

---

[5] As numbered and arranged by Diels.
[6] This phraseology is derived from the Eleatic discussions: Anaxagoras here asserts the continuity of Being, in which each thing (phenomenon) has not absolute, but relative, magnitude.

all other animals, as many as have Psyche (Life, Soul). And these human beings possess inhabited cities and cultivated fields, just as among us; and they have a sun and a moon and the other heavenly bodies, just as among us, and their earth brings forth for them many things and every sort of thing; of these they gather the best together into their dwellings and use them. All this I have said about the separation, to show that not only in our case has there been a separation [of a universe], but also elsewhere. Before the separation took place, when all things were together, there was not even any color to be seen, for the mixture of all things prevented, the mixture of moist and dry, of hot and cold, of bright and dark, and of much earth that was in it, and of a quantity of infinite Seeds that were in no way like each other. For not a single one of all the other things is like any other. Since these things are so, we must think that all things are present in the sum of Being.

(5) And after these things have been thus separated, we must know that the sum of all things is neither smaller nor greater, for it is impossible that there should be more than the sum of all things; but the sum of Being is always equal.

(6) And since the portions of the great and of the small are equal in quantity, for this reason also all things must be in every thing; for all things cannot be apart, but all things have a part of every thing. Since the [absolutely] smallest thing cannot exist, it could not be separated, nor could it come into being by itself; but as it was in the beginning so even now all things are together. Many things are present in all things, and they are equal in quantity, both in the greater and in the smaller of those things that are separated off.

(7) The result is that we cannot know the quantity of the things that are separated off, either by reason or by doing anything.

(8) The things that are in one universe are not separated from each other, nor are they cut off by an axe, neither hot from cold nor cold from hot.

(9) . . . When these things revolve in this way and are separated by force and swiftness. And the swiftness is the cause of the force. The swiftness of these things is not at all like the swiftness of anything that there now is among men, but is certainly many times as swift.

(10) For how can hair come into being out of what is not hair, and flesh out of what is not flesh?

(11) In every thing there is a portion of every thing, except of Mind (πλὴν νοῦ), and in some things Mind also is present.

(12) Other things have a portion of every thing; but Mind is infinite and has sovereign power and is mixed with no thing, but is alone, itself by itself. For if it were not by itself, but were mixed with anything else, it would have a part of all things if it were mixed with any thing; for there is a part of every thing in every thing, as I have said in what goes before; and the things that would be mixed wtih Mind would hinder its action, so that it could not be supreme over anything in the same way that it is now when it is alone and by itself. For Mind is the most subtle of all things and the purest, and it possesses all knowledge about everything and has the greatest strength. And as many things as have Psyche, both smaller and greater things, all have Mind for their supreme ruler. And Mind was supreme over the whole revolution, so that the revolution took place in the beginning. And the movement of revolution began with that which was small, and it revolves over a greater space, and it will revolve over still more space. And Mind knew all the things that were mingled and separated and distinguished. And all the sorts of things that were to be and that were, including all those that do not now exist, and all the sorts that do now exist, all these Mind arranged into a universe, and it also arranged this movement of revolution in which the stars now revolve and the sun and the moon and the Air and the Aither, that are separated. It is this very movement of revolution that made them separate. And dense is separate from rare, and hot from cold, and bright from dark, and dry

from moist. And there are many parts of many things; but nothing is wholly separated or distinguished from anything else except Mind. And Mind is all alike, both the greater and the smaller Mind. But nothing else is like anything else; but each one thing is and was most visible as being that of which it has the greatest quantity in it.

(13) And when Mind began to set things in motion, it was separated from all that was moved, and everything that Mind set in motion was rendered wholly distinct; and as things were set in motion and rendered distinct, the movement of revolution caused their distinctness to become much greater.

(14) And Mind [and all things that are] is certainly even now where all other things are,[7] namely in the great containing envelope, and in the things that have been combined, and in the things that have been separated.

(15) The thick, moist, cold and dark gathered in that place where they now are, and the thin, hot and dry went out to the further part of the Aither.

(16) From these as they are separated earth is put firmly together; for water is separated out of the clouds, and earth out of the water, and out of the earth stones are put firmly together by the agency of cold, and these stones proceed further out than water.

(17) The Greeks do not have the correct notion about becoming and perishing; for nothing comes into being or perishes, but there is only mixture and separation out of things that exist. And thus they might rightly call becoming a mixture, and perishing a separation.

(21) By reason of the weakness of our senses we have not the power to form true judgments.

(21a) The things which appear [i.e., phenomena] are a revelation of that which cannot be seen.

---

[7] The MSS. of Simplicius read ὁ δὲ νοῦς ὅσα ἐστί τε κάρτα καὶ νῦν ἐστιν, ἵνα κα τὰ ἄλλα πάντα . . . The easiest solution is probably to assume that τε should be placed after ὅσα. Anaxagoras locates Mind in the great containing envelope, which consists of the finest and most remote Aither (see next fragment).

(21b) By experience, memory, skill and craftsmanship we are able to make use of the other animals.

Simplicius says (*Phys.*, 27, 2) that Anaxagoras "shared the philosophical beliefs of Anaximenes," and all the available evidence confirms this statement. Archelaos, who was a disciple of Anaxagoras, taught that "infinite Air was the first cause, and its contraction and expansion; and of these things that expand and contract, one is Fire and the other is water" (*FV*, 47 A 7); and both Anaxagoras and Archelaos taught that "Psyche (Soul, Life) is made of Air" (*FV*, 46 A 93). And Aristotle informs us that Anaxagoras says that "Psyche is the moving principle" (*De Anima*, 404 a 25). "In many places," says Aristotle (404 b), "Anaxagoras speaks of Mind as the cause of the good and the true, but elsewhere he says that Mind and Psyche are the same thing, for he says that Mind exists in all living beings, both large and small, precious and less valuable." So far, the supreme god of Anaxagoras is identical with the supreme god of Anaximenes, which was infinite and indeterminate, but also definite (ὡρισμένος) Air, and which was Psyche, the cause of Life, in all living beings great and small, including the gods and the universe itself.

The starting-point and the general essence of the doctrine of Anaxagoras are therefore the same as in the case of Anaximenes. But when we inspect the fragments which survive from the book of Anaxagoras, we are at once struck by the presence of a number of novel phrases and ideas which do not at first sight appear consistent either with one another or with the philosophy of Anaximenes. What does Anaxagoras mean by "the small" and "the great"? What are the "things" (χρήματα) and the "Seeds" (σπέρματα)? How can Mind be "not mixed with anything," and yet be "present in some things"? How can Mind be "in the great containing envelope of Aither"?

These difficulties may be considerably diminished if we resolve to employ the same method of interpretation that applies to every philosopher except Thales, and that does not apply to Thales only because he had no one to contradict. Many of these puzzling affirmative statements are really negations, and they need simply to be put back into negative form; once that is done, we shall be able to see what Anaxagoras really meant, so far as a negation can have a real meaning.

Anaxagoras starts by accepting the essential Unity of Being, as we should expect of a follower of Thales, Anaximander, and Anaximenes, and he emphasizes the infinity of Being or of Substance or of those "things which were together," in orthodox obedience to the doctrine of Anaximenes. But here comes a novelty; we learn that infinity is specified both of the number and of the smallness of the things that were together. Applying our principle, we must inquire who had said that "things were together, but were limited in number and in smallness"; it is clear enough that this would be a fairly good statement of the doctrine of Empedocles, with his six gods who were "together" in (Strife was on the edge of) the Sphairos. From the point of view of Anaxagoras, Empedocles had taken six discontinuous divine powers and had put them forcibly together; Anaxagoras denies that they were six, and denies that they were discontinuous, and asserts the absolute supremacy of Air and Aither. The terms by which he denies discontinuity are disconcerting to our ears: the statement that "the small is infinite" is not our way of affirming the continuity of Being: but if we look at Fragment 3, and compare it with Fragments 6 and 8, we can see how Anaxagoras carried out his argument. "There is no smallest of that which is small, but there is always a smaller; for Being cannot be non-being" (3) is the Greek way of saying that there are no absolutely smallest discrete plural units which make up Being; for if such units be imagined, it is clear that none of them will be absolutely smallest as long as any interval remains to separate it from complete nothingness or non-being. Zeno of Elea employed the same argument when he said that "if What Is had no magnitude, it would not even be" (*FV*, 19 B 1). Since there is no smallest thing, the things that are "are not [absolutely] separated from each other, nor are they cut off by an axe" (8); and henceforth, whenever we find Anaxagoras using the terms "separate" and "distinguished" and "not mixed," we must remember that he uses them subject to this metaphysical proviso. If he had permitted anything to be "cut off by an axe," that thing would straightway have become a completely separate entity, whether it were great or small; and the whole system of Anaxagoras is a protest against all attempts to introduce discontinuity into Being, and especially against the attempt of Empedocles.

But if there is no discontinuity, how can Air and Aither be named, in Fragment 1, as the two things that are supreme over everything else? And above all, how can Anaxagoras, who has asserted the absolute continuity of Being, in strict obedience to the Milesian doctrine that the supreme god was the one causal substance of all Being, venture to proclaim in Fragment 12 that Mind (Nous) is the supreme ruler? We now have three supreme rulers of the universe, which seems a more than adequate supply for a philosopher who opposes Empedocles on the ground that he was guilty of splitting up Being with an axe. In comparison with this puzzle, all the other difficulties in the interpretation of Anaxagoras sink into insignificance. Before we attempt to solve this puzzle, we may derive a little consolation from examining the evidence of Plato and of Aristotle, who were alternately delighted and disgusted by Anaxagoras, and accused him of thinking inconsistently.

The views of Plato are stated by Socrates in the *Phaedo*, 97 and 98. Socrates has just been saying that when he was young he was very eager to know that department of philosophy which investigates nature, "as being the science which teaches how to know the causes of each thing, why it comes into being, why it perishes, and why it is." Socrates accordingly had studied various doctrines, but had become disgusted with them all, and had begun to form a confused notion of a method of his own. "Then I heard some one read out of a book which was, he said, by Anaxagoras, that 'Mind forms the universe and is the Cause of all things,' and I was delighted with this cause, and I decided that Mind must really be in some sense the cause of all things. If this is so, I thought, the Mind that is the source of universal Order must arrange each particular thing in the best possible way . . . and I rejoiced to think that I had found in Anaxagoras a man who would teach me about such a cause. . . . I would not have sold my expectations even at a great price, but seized his books enthusiastically and read as fast as I could, in order to know at once the truth about what is better and what is worse. Farewell to my marvellous hopes! As I went on with my reading, I beheld a man who made no use whatever of Mind, who ascribed to it no rôle in the production of cosmic order, but who on the contrary ascribed all causal action to Airs, and Aithers, and Waters, and many other strange things." Plato again returned to the charge, in the *Laws*, 967 b-d: "Even at that time some ventured to guess that Mind was the source of all order in those things which are in the sky; but they failed to discover the true nature of Psyche and its precedence over bodies, and upset the universe, or rather themselves, by deciding that body had precedence over Psyche, for they judged by appearances and thought that the sky was full of whirling stones and earth and many other lifeless bodies."

Aristotle follows Plato in expressing the same delight and the same profound disappointment. "When one man said, then, that Mind was present, just as in animals, also in nature, as the Cause of the universe and of all this Order, he seemed like a sober man in contrast with the random [drunken] talk of his predecessors" (*Met.*, 984 b 15). "Earlier thinkers make almost no use of their causes: for Anaxagoras uses Mind as a *deus ex machina* in the formation of the universe, and when he does not know for what reason something necessarily is, then he drags in Mind, but in all other cases he ascribes causal power over becoming to anything rather than to Mind" (*Met.*, 985 a 17). It will be noticed that Aristotle is much more unkind to Anaxagoras than Plato was: Plato merely says that Anaxagoras, after naming Mind, actually ascribed all causality to Airs, Aithers, and Waters, while Aristotle implies that Anaxagoras never names Mind except when he is trying to conceal his ignorance.

If we disregard the rudeness of Aristotle, on the ground that it is only one more example of the way in which great men habitually abuse their predecessors rather than make the mental effort of forming a just historical estimate, the only definite information that we can derive from these passages is that which Plato gives us: Mind is once mentioned by Anaxagoras as the cause of all things, and thereafter all causality is ascribed to Airs, Aithers, and Waters. Are we to assume that Anaxagoras believed in four causes? That would certainly be a counsel of despair. On the contrary, let us try to imagine that we too are followers of Anaximenes, and that we are attempting to restate our master's philosophy under the conditions that are imposed by the intellectual atmosphere of the middle of the fifth century B.C. We have been much impressed by the criticism of Parmenides, and to it we shall make such concessions as in Fragments 5 and 17; the sum of Being, though infinite, is always equal, and there is no real becoming or perishing. But that is the limit of our generosity, and we are determined to reassert the doctrine of our master, that the supreme divine power, the source of all Life in temporary individual beings as well as in the cosmos, is Air. Just as Anaximenes did not hesitate to compare our own Psyche, "which is Air," to the Pneuma and Air that "contains" the whole universe, so we also shall affirm that the Psyche is made of Air, and shall not hesitate to refer to the one divine substance out of which the universe proceeds by the two names of Air and Aither. Air is cold and Aither is hot, but we regard Air and Aither as but two aspects of the same single power; and we are quite certain about this, because Anaximenes proved it (Plutarch, *De Prim. Frig.*, 7, 947 F). When he breathed with his mouth open, the Air was hot and rare; but when he expelled his breath forcibly through lips pressed together as for whistling, the Air was cold and dense. We are therefore free to apply two names to our supreme divine power without in the least becoming dualists in our philosophy; the suggestion would strike us as absurd. And if we so desire, we shall go on enumerating different aspects of the supreme divine power, precisely as Heraclitus successively identified his supreme god with the One, Psyche, Harmonia, Logos (Reason), Fastening, Destiny, and Law, without ever for one moment abandoning his conviction that the supreme god was Fire.

But we do not desire to multiply interminably the attributes of our one greatest god, and for a very good reason. Empedocles has just introduced four unalterable discontinuous deities —discontinuous in the sense that they are really units of separate and immutable substances—and has joined to them two other gods, Strife and Love, one of whom is a Devil and the other an incomprehensible (to us) cause of Unity. We believe in the partial reality of change, but not at the cost of supporting such a passionate religious philosophy as that of Empedocles, with its variegated and discontinuous deities. What shall we do? We will affirm that there is one continuous power that makes the universe, and that Air and Aither, which we regard as that one power, may and must be called by that title which best asserts the perfection of our supreme god, since perfection must not be sullied by the passions of Love and Strife. Therefore we say that our supreme god is Mind (Nous).

In some such way Anaxagoras must have reached his conclusion. When we have once dismissed the false and unhistorical notion that Anaxagoras set up the divinity of Mind apart from physical substance, without realizing that he had substituted a sudden dualism for the Ionian doctrine of the one divine substance, we can return to his doctrines with a reasonable chance of understanding them. Air and Aither were supreme when all things were together (1); so also was Mind (12). When all things were together, all the opposites were in the mixture, and in particular a quantity of infinite Seeds (4). These Seeds are not atoms, nor are they "elements," as has been asserted: Anaxagoras believes in continuity, and in one "element" and not in many. They stand simply for the power of creating Life that is one of the endowments of the supreme god; and we find Theophrastus (*FV*, 46 A 117) recording the assertion of Anaxagoras "that the Air has Seeds of all things, and that when these Seeds are carried down by the water they produce plants." Anaxagoras also taught that plants are alive, that they have feelings and emotions, and that they think and reason. Therefore plants share that Mind which is Air and Psyche, the source of all Life and Thought. What then does Anaxagoras mean by saying that "Mind is mixed with no thing, but is alone, itself by itself"? In the same Fragment (12), we learn that "nothing is wholly separate from anything else except Mind," and in Fragment 11, that "Mind is present in some things."

These apparent contradictions are due to the fact that Mind, the supreme god Air and Aither, is in general separate from its own lowest forms, with the result that those lowest forms are not living, and have no Psyche present within them. Heraclitus established the same distinction between Fire and the lowest forms of Fire, but Anaxagoras has altered the metaphor of the Way Down that was traversed by divine Fire, and has represented his supreme god as initiating a movement of revolution in a circle ever widening (περιχωρήσει ἐπὶ πλέον, 12), by which the god itself is separated further and further from its own lower forms, all of which it knows and arranges and rules with sovereign power. During this movement of revolution (περιχώρησις), earth is condensed at the center of the universe, out of the dense and moist and dark and cold opposites

[113]

that are peculiarly attributes of Air, and the centrifugal force
that is developed by the inconceivable speed of the motion of
Mind causes "stones" to detach themselves from earth and to
be flung into the sky, where they are heated and sustained by
the revolving divine Fire that Anaxagoras calls Aither. It was
this feature of his doctrine, which of course he did not in the
least intend as an impiety, that brought upon him the condemnation of the Athenians, who believed in 431 B.C. exactly what
they had believed for several centuries, that sun and moon
and stars were gods. We should remember that hitherto every
philosopher or scientist of whom we have any record had coun-
tenanced this popular belief, and that Pythagoras and his followers had given to the stars, sun, moon and planets an especially high degree of divinity by generating them directly out
of his central divine Fire.

When the movement of revolution is once established, Mind
continues its task of separating first itself and then all the lower
forms of itself into distinct "things," which are the phenomena
that we see, and are also, if we have the eyes of Anaxagoras, a
"revelation of things unseen" (21 a), that is to say a revelation
of Air and Aither and Mind, the unseen supreme divine power
which is visible only in phenomena, and which the portion of
Mind that is in us can behold only dimly, since its perfect vision
is hindered by the imperfect senses (21). But phenomena,
"things," are constantly changing under the operation of supreme Mind or Air or Aither. That is, the lower forms of
Air and Aither are thought of as a continuous substance, which
cannot really be divided, but which can be arranged by Mind,
and every rearrangement produces new phenomena, upon which
men bestow separate names in accordance with what might be
called the dominant pattern of the rearrangement. These pat-
terns are what we recognize as qualitative differences, as "hair"
and "flesh" (10), but in every case the visible qualitative difference has been produced out of the invisible divine substance,
which is susceptible of an infinite number of rearrangements,
and therefore may be spoken of as being potentially anything,

including hair and flesh, and thereby differs from the discontinuous four elemental gods of Empedocles, when those four gods are judged and rejected from the hostile point of view of Anaxagoras. That is what Anaxagoras means by Fragment 10; if Empedocles were right, a bone would be produced when Love mixes two parts of Nestis (Water) with four of Hephaistos (Fire) and two of Earth. But Anaxagoras refuses to believe that a bone can come out of substances that are completely discontinuous and distinct; hence he asks how hair "can come into being out of what is not hair." Underneath all external qualitative differences, there lies the internal continuity of a substance of which the source is the supreme god; and the continuity of these lower substances is but the translation, into the language of phenomena, of the divine Unity of Air and Aither, of which the highest attribute is Mind. Aristotle described this continuity, in his own terms, by saying that the "elements" employed by Anaxagoras were things of "like parts," homoeomeries (ὁμοιομερῆ); but since there was in the system of Anaxagoras only one real "element," and all diversity was due to the infinite number of aspects which that supreme god was capable of assuming, it would be better to use in discussing Anaxagoras terms that are less liable to misunderstanding.

What contribution did Anaxagoras make to the kaleidoscopic alterations in the doctrine of the supreme god that have so far constituted the movement of Greek philosophy? Under the stimulus of that desire for a more nearly perfect definition of the supreme god, the effects of which have been manifest in so many diverse doctrines, Anaxagoras offered a new solution of the Eleatic difficulty. His supreme god, Life-Mind-Air-Aither, the "most subtle of all things and the purest" (12), is the infinite sovereign power, and out of its substance proceed all the things that we call phenomena. This universe therefore is a Unity, in spite of the fact that Anaxagoras regards change as real; and when Anaxagoras is emphasizing Unity, he asserts, as in Fragment 1, that "all things were together," and that "nothing is cut off by an axe" (8), and proclaims, as in Fragment 21a, that phenomena are not mere unrealities divorced from the supreme god, but are a genuine revelation of things unseen. Furthermore, his supreme god has no Limits such as confined the Being of Parmenides, but has the creative liberty which belongs to Life, and exercises it by creating other universes, each of which will be essentially a unit, but all of which, even when regarded as coexisting, will not mar the infinite Unity of Mind.

Anaxagoras has thus managed to restore to the supreme god the Life and power over change of which it had been robbed by Parmenides; he is now compelled to invent an answer to the Eleatic doctrine that all change and all movement are blots upon the perfection of the supreme god. This answer is Mind. Mind is the source of all change, Mind is the cause of all movement; and since Mind is a perfect cause, who shall dare assail it? When Anaxagoras is dealing with the definition of Mind, he dwells upon its solitary and omnipotent perfection;[8] it "has all knowledge about everything and has the greatest strength," it is separated and distinguished from everything else, in order to guarantee its pure perfection. Furthermore, this can be proved; in the universe as we know it, Air and Aither actually are separated and distinguished from everything else, as Anaxagoras says in Fragments 2 and 12. They have attained this separation by their own creative circular movement. With Mind endowed with these attributes, Anaxagoras rested content, so far as Eleatic criticism was concerned.

Be it said to his honor, Anaxagoras did not remain contented when once he had set up a definition that seemed to him perfect, but also paid some attention to facts. Facts demonstrated that somehow or other the "sovereign" power of Mind was limited, and that a subtraction must be made from its omnipotence. At

[8] For this reason, Anaxagoras speaks of Mind (12) as "wholly separate." But "no thing is cut off by an axe." The two statements are logically inconsistent, but that does not prove that Anaxagoras did not believe in a single ultimate reality, or that Mind and Aither are not the same. The inconsistency is precisely parallel to that committed by Heraclitus, when he affirmed that dead bodies were contemptible: and yet all things were forms of the one perfect reality, which was Fire.

the other end of the continuous scale that led from Mind downward to its products, there were things that had no Mind in them, and were therefore lifeless, and could not move themselves, but could only be moved from without, by Mind-Air-Aither or by its nearest agents on the way down to the centre of the universe. Situated on this scale, there were things called plants, which lived, and therefore must have within them a portion of Mind itself, and above the plants were the other animals and man. In all these living things, Mind was present, and yet obviously Mind was hampered, limited, impaired, in different degrees; animals devoured, with complete impunity, plants in which there was a portion of the supreme god; and man has subjugated, and is now able to exploit, many other animals, because he is the most intelligent animal (21 b); and man is the most intelligent animal, not because the Mind in him is different from Mind elsewhere, but because he alone has hands (Aristotle, *De Part. An.*, Δ, 10, 687 a 7). Anaxagoras thus found himself compelled to recognize the inferiority of stone and earth, the substances which were at the bottom of the scale, and the inferiority of the bodies which surround Mind in plants and animals, as being opposed to the perfection and the sovereignty of Mind. Only in the case of man was body so arranged as to permit the Mind in him a limited freedom; and even in man the senses are so imperfect that Mind is crippled.

In the system of Anaxagoras, Mind has created out of itself an infinite substance of infinite mutability, and this substance, though continuous with Mind, is nevertheless to a certain degree opposed to Mind. This substance, in the lower parts of the scale of perfection, may be called "body," but it should be noted that it does not at all resemble the immutable discontinuous four gods of Empedocles; and it appears to have had little or no effect upon scientific ideas. But the notion of divine Mind as the source of all order in the universe, though it was not a novelty, was very clearly outlined by Anaxagoras, and had great influence upon Plato, Aristotle, and the Stoics.

CHAPTER XI

THE ATOMISTS

L EUCIPPUS was a member of the school of Parmenides at Elea, where he is said to have listened to the lectures of Zeno. We have no other definite information about the life of Leucippus, except that he founded the philosophy of the Atomists, which was taught by his pupil Democritus at Abdera in Thrace. Democritus, who appears to have been born a few years later than Socrates (about 460 B.C.), was one of the most copious authors in all antiquity. Of his books, only fragments remain, for the most part moral maxims; of the books of Leucippus, we have one sentence left, from the *Treatise on Mind*: "No thing comes into being at random, but all things come from Reason and through the action of Necessity" (*FV*, 54 B 2).

Empedocles and Anaxagoras had in their various ways tried to affirm the reality of change without abandoning what seemed to them the most valuable attributes of Parmenidean Being. But Leucippus risked his philosophic life on a far bolder doctrine; he began by accepting the direct challenge issued by Parmenides himself in the Way of Truth (*FV*, 18 B 6): "for Being is, and non-being is not; this I bid you to think over, and I restrain you from this first way of investigation." We have already seen that "this first way of investigation" was the way of Pythagoras, and that Parmenides denounced the dispersion of the One in the multitude of microcosms, separated from each other by the void, as amounting to the destruction of Being. Hence, rather than admit the discontinuity of Being, Parmenides had gone to the extreme of denying the reality of phenomena and of the void which separates phenomena. Now

Leucippus asserts that he can preserve the reality of phenomena, and of the void which separates them, without destroying the perfection of Being. So far from destroying the perfection of Being, Leucippus will enhance it; from his point of
view, the fact that Parmenidean Being is motionless is not a
perfection but an imperfection, and the fact that Parmenidean
Being has only one Form is also an imperfection, since it prevents Being from exercising its causal function not only over
other universes, but over everything in this universe except the
total spherical Form of this universe. Therefore Leucippus im-
proves the supreme god of Parmenides by restoring to it the
attribute of motion, and by dividing it into an infinite number
of Forms. Each one of these Forms is in itself absolutely full of
Being, perfect and immutable exactly as was the One Being
of Parmenides; each Form is a genuine Cause of phenomena;
and the variety of different Forms is infinite, since the variety
of phenomena which they cause is infinite.

When we turn to the accounts of this doctrine given by
ancient writers, we must be prepared to make allowances for
the inevitable distortion that it undergoes in being reported by
philosophers who were members of other schools. Even Epicurus, who owed a great debt to Leucippus and to Democritus, and should have been correspondingly grateful, not only
did not acknowledge his debt, but denied "the very existence
of Leucippus the philosopher" (Diogenes Laertius, X, 13);
and this convenient method of cancelling indebtedness by
annihilating the creditor has been taken seriously by two
modern historians.[1]

Simplicius says (*Phys.*, 28, 4):

"Leucippus of Elea or of Miletus (both accounts are given)
shared his philosophy with Parmenides, but did not follow the
same method that Parmenides and Xenophanes followed in the
explanation of things that are, but, as it appears, the opposite
method. They had represented the All as One, Immovable,
Eternal, and Limited, and did not permit even the investiga-

[1] Rohde and Brieger.

tion of non-being; Leucippus assumed Infinite and forever
Moving elements, the Indivisible Beings, and an Infinite number of Forms among them, because there is no real difference
in quality in any phenomenon, and because he saw incessant
coming into being and change in things that are. Moreover,
Being does not exist any more really than non-being, and both
are alike causes of that which comes into being. For he assumed
that the Being of the Indivisible Beings was Compact and
Full, and he called it What Is (Being) and said that it moved
in the void, which he called non-being and which he said
existed no less than Being. And similarly his comrade Democritus of Abdera established the Full and the void as first principles, and called one of them Being and the other non-being;
for Leucippus and Democritus assume the Indivisible Beings
as the matter of things that are, and by the differences in the
Beings they produce everything else. These differences are
three, Form (ῥυσμός), Turning (τροπή), and Contact (δια-
θιγή), and they have the same meaning as Shape (σχῆμα),
Position (θέσις), and Arrangement (τάξις). For by nature
like things are moved by like things, and things that are akin
rush together, and each of the Forms, when it is arranged in a
different combination of Forms, produces a different arrangement; so that they claimed with good reason that since these
first principles were Infinite they would produce all substances
and all modifications of them, accounting both for the cause
of everything that comes into being and for the manner in
which it comes. Wherefore they even make the claim that only
those philosophers who represent the elements as Infinite can
argue that all things take place in accordance with Reason.
And they say that the number of Forms, among the Indivisible
Beings, is Infinite, because there is no real difference in quality
in anything. This, they say, is the cause of infinity" (i.e., of
the infinitely different qualities apparent in phenomena, which
qualities do not really exist).

Aristotle, in his treatise *De Generatione et Corruptione*
(315 a 34), is highly complimentary to Leucippus and De-

mocritus: "In general no one made any more than a superficial inquiry into these problems, except Democritus; he seems to have studied them all, and is far superior in his method. For, as we are saying, none of the other philosophers made any definite statement about growth, except such as any amateur might have made; they said that things grow when like joins like, but they did not explain the process, nor did they give any account of combination, or of any of the other problems, such as action and passion, how in all actions in nature one thing acts and another is acted upon. But Democritus and Leucippus assume the Forms and make alteration and coming-to-be result from them; they explain coming-to-be and perishing by the dispersion and the union of the Forms, and alteration by their arrangement and position. And since they thought that the truth lay in the appearance, and the appearances are opposite and infinite, they made the Forms Infinite, so that by reason of the changes in any compound the same thing presents opposite appearances to different people; its movement changes when a small addition is made to it, and it appears totally different when the position of one thing is changed. For tragedy and comedy both come to be out of the same letters. . . . If things that are are magnitudes, are they bodies, as in the system of Democritus and Leucippus, or are they planes, as in the *Timaeus*? . . . The rival treatments of this subject illustrate the great difference between the method of natural science and the method of dialectical inquiry: for the Platonists argue that magnitudes are indivisible because 'otherwise the Formal Triangle will be many'; but Democritus appears to have been convinced of this by arguments that were appropriate and were drawn from natural science (325 a 23). . . . Leucippus thought that he had a system which harmonized with sense-perception and which would not do away with coming-to-be or perishing or motion and the multiplicity of things. So much he conceded to phenomena; and then he conceded to those who maintain the One that there could be no motion without void: hence he asserts that the void is non-being, and that no part of Being is non-being, since real Being is completely Full. But he goes on to say that the Full is not one, but is Infinite in number and quantity, and is Invisible owing to the smallness of the sizes. These move in the void (for there is a void); and when they unite they cause coming-to-be and when they separate they cause perishing. They act and are acted upon in so far as they are in contact, for in this respect they are not one, and they generate when they are put together and intertwined (325 b 17). . . . The primary 'bodies' of Leucippus are Indivisible, and differ only in Shape (326 a). . . . Leucippus and Democritus must hold that each of the Indivisibles is impassive [incapable of receiving a sensible property], for nothing can be acted upon except through the void, and must also hold that each Indivisible is incapable of producing a sensible property,[2] for no Indivisible can be for example hard or cold. And yet it is surely strange that they attribute heat exclusively to the Spherical Form; for if that is so cold must belong to another Form. And further, it is strange that heat and cold should belong to the Indivisibles, but that heaviness and lightness, hardness and softness, should not belong to them. And yet Democritus says that each of the Indivisibles is heavier according to its excess[3] [of solid, cf. *De Caelo*, 309 a 14]. . . . But certainly it is strange that no property except Form should belong to the Indivisibles . . . Moreover it is strange that there should be only small Indivisibles, and no large ones."

Diogenes Laertius contributes an account of the formation of universes (IX, 31):

"The All is Infinite; part of it is Full, and part of it void, and these he calls elements. From these the infinite universes are derived and into them they are dissolved. In this way

___

[2] On the contrary, they actually held that the Indivisibles were capable of producing every sensible quality.

[3] Democritus of course said nothing of the sort; this is merely an example of the way in which Aristotle very often attributes to other philosophers opinions which are obvious fabrications of his own. He intended them as demonstrations of the absurdities implicit in other systems than his own. Unfortunately, this passage was taken seriously by Theophrastus, and thus the imaginary problem, whether Atoms have weight as an original property, was created. Just below, Aristotle admits that no property except Form belongs to the Indivisibles.

the universes come into being: many 'bodies' of all sorts of Shapes are cut off from the Infinite and rush into a great void; these gather together and form a single revolution, in which they jostle and revolve in every way, and finally separate, like joining like. And since owing to the crowd they can no longer revolve in equilibrium, the fine Shapes depart to the outer void, as if sifted out; the rest stay together and becoming entangled run down together with each other and form a kind of first spherical system.[4] This system separates as a sort of membrane, containing within it all kinds of bodies; and as they revolve, by reason of the resistance of the center the surrounding membrane becomes thin, as the contiguous bodies always combine owing to their contact in the revolution. Thus the earth is formed, as that which has been carried towards the center remains together. Then the containing membrane grows as bodies outside flow to it; and since it is itself revolving, it adds to itself whatever it touches. Some of these cohere and form a system, at first damp and muddy, but when they have dried and revolve with the revolution of the whole system, they take fire and form the substance of the Stars. The orbit of the Sun is outermost, that of the Moon is nearest to the earth; the orbits of the rest lie between these."

On Psyche, we have Aristotle, *De Anima*, 404 a:

"There are some who maintain that Psyche is preeminently and primarily the cause of movement. . . . Hence Democritus says that Psyche is a sort of Fire or Heat, for the Shapes and Indivisibles are Infinite and he calls those which are Spherical, Fire and Psyche; they resemble the so-called motes in the air, which are visible in the sunbeams that enter through our windows; the mixture of all Seeds [made out of these Spherical Shapes] he calls the elements of all nature, and Leucippus agrees. And those which have a Spherical Form are Psyche, since such Forms can most easily penetrate everything, and being themselves in motion, can most easily move everything else; since Leucippus and Democritus assume that

---

[4] Leucippus seems to have used σύστημα to mean a kind of organic combination.

Psyche imparts motion to all living beings. Hence they represent respiration as that which determines life; for as that which surrounds the bodies of animals presses upon them and squeezes out those Forms which, because they are never at rest themselves, impart motion to living beings, help comes from outside, as other such Forms enter in in respiration. For these Spherical Forms prevent the Forms that are already present in the animals from being driven out, since they keep in check that which presses upon and solidifies bodies. And life continues as long as there is strength to do this. The doctrine of the Pythagoreans seems also to contain the same thought. . . . Democritus absolutely identified Psyche and Mind, and held that the truth is that which appears [to the senses]. . . ."[5]

The commentary of Philoponus on the *De Anima* says (83, 27):

"Democritus said that Fire was incorporeal, not absolutely incorporeal (for none of them meant this), but as that which, among bodies, was incorporeal because of its subtlety."

A few passages deal with the theory of knowledge and with the gods:

"Leucippus and Democritus say that sensations and thoughts are alterations of the body. . . . Sensation and thought arise when images ($\epsilon\check{\iota}\delta\omega\lambda\alpha$) approach from without" (*FV*, 54 A 30).

"The others say that those things which are perceived by the senses exist by nature, but Leucippus, Democritus and Diogenes say that they exist by convention ($\nu\acute{o}\mu\dot{\varphi}$), that is by opinion and by our sensations. Nothing is true or comprehensible except the first elements, the Indivisibles and void. These alone exist by nature, but the things perceived by the senses are non-essential qualities derived from those elements, and differ on account of the Position, Arrangement and Shape of the Indivisibles" (*FV*, 54 A 32).

---

[5] The first part of this statement is true; the second is an opinion constructed by Aristotle to show that the theory of Democritus would lead to this absurd consequence, as Zeller pointed out. In the *De Generatione et Corruptione*, 315 b 9, Aristotle stated the doctrine correctly.

THE ATOMISTS

"Leucippus and Democritus think that images flow off, of like form with that from which they flow, and fall into the eyes of those who see, and thus vision arises" (*FV*, 54 A 29).

"You cannot possibly adopt the opinion laid down by the revered judgment of great Democritus, that the first-beginnings of body and of Mind are placed one beside one alternately in pairs, and so link the frame together" (Lucretius, III, 370-3).

"Democritus says that all things partake of some sort of Psyche (Life), even those 'bodies' that are dead, since they always visibly partake of something warm and endowed with sensation, that penetrates the greater part with its Breath" (*FV*, 55 A 117).

"Democritus and some others say that the elements have Psychai (Lives, Souls) and that these are the causes of the birth of stones, for he says that there is Psyche in a stone just as in any other Seed which brings anything into being, and that the Heat of the matter within is a cause of motion in the birth of a stone, just as a hammer is moved by a smith to produce an axe or a saw" (*FV*, 55 A 164).

"Democritus annihilates those things that appear to the senses, and says that nothing appears as it truly is but only as it is thought to be, but that truth is to be found in the realities, in the existence of the Indivisibles and void; for 'by convention,' he says, 'there is sweet, by convention bitter, by convention hot, by convention cold, by convention color: but in truth there are Indivisibles and void. . . . We ourselves in reality understand nothing exactly, but only as it changes according to the disposition of our body and of the things that enter into it and of the things that resist.'. . . And in the treatise *On Forms* (Περὶ ἰδεῶν), 'We must recognize,' he says, 'a human being by this rule, namely that he is far from the truth. . . . And this reasoning also makes it clear that in truth we know nothing about anything, but for each of us his opinion is an afflux [of images]. . . . There are two Forms (ἰδέαι) of Knowledge, one legitimate, the other bastard; to bastard knowledge belong all these things, sight, hearing, smell, taste, touch; but legitimate knowledge is separated from this.'. . . Diotimus said that according to Democritus there were three criteria: that phenomena were the criterion for the comprehension of things unseen (for phenomena are 'a revelation of things invisible,' as Anaxagoras says, whom Democritus praises for this doctrine); that the concept was the criterion of investigation (for 'concerning every topic, my boy, there is one beginning, i.e. to know what the investigation concerns'); and that sense-experiences were the criterion of choice and avoidance (for that to which we are close kin must be chosen, and that to which we are alien must be avoided)." (Sextus Empiricus, VII, 135-40).

"Plato and Democritus both supposed that only the objects of thought really existed: Democritus believed this because there was no sensible substance underlying nature, since the Indivisibles which formed all things by their combinations had a nature devoid of all sensible quality; and Plato believed this because the objects of sense-perception were always coming-to-be but never were, since Being flowed like a river, so that the same thing never abode for two of the least units of time" (Sextus Empiricus, VIII, 6, 7).

"Whatsoever a poet writes with God present within him and with the holy Pneuma (Spirit or Breath) is very beautiful" (*FV*, 55 B 18).

"Healthful Reason, which is the Sun of the Psyche, can alone, when it has risen within the depth of the Mind, illuminate the eye of the Psyche: whence Democritus quite rightly says that 'a few men, who possess Reason, stretch out their hands towards that which we Greeks now call Air and address it as Zeus; for Zeus knows all things, gives and takes away all things, and is King of all things.' " (*FV*, 55 B 30).[6]

"Happiness does not dwell in herds of cattle nor in gold: Psyche is the abode of deity" (*FV*, 55 B 171).

---

[6] This has been interpreted as a piece of sarcasm: it is of course a serious statement of a serious theological belief. It is entirely consistent with the theology of Leucippus and Democritus: Air was akin to Fire, and Fire was God.

"The gods give all good things to men, both of old and now. But neither of old nor now do the gods give to men what is evil, harmful, and useless, but men bring these things upon themselves on account of the blindness and the ignorance of their minds" (*FV*, 55 B 175).

"Only those who hate to do wrong are dear to the gods" (*FV*, 55 B 217).

"A wise man may travel to every land; for the whole universe is the native country of a wise Psyche" (*FV*, 55 B 247).

"Images draw near to human beings, and some of these do good and some do evil (wherefore Democritus prayed that he might have the fortune to meet happy images), and they are great and marvellous, and they are almost but not quite Imperishable, and they foretell coming events to human beings, being visible and speaking. Wherefore men of old, perceiving these images, imagined that each was a god, although God in reality is only that which has Imperishable Nature" (*FV*, 55 B 166).

"Democritus says that Mind is God, and is in Fire of Spherical Form (Cicero, *De Deor. Nat.*, 1, 12, 29).... What of Democritus, who now counts as gods images which travel about, and now that Nature which pours forth and sends out these images, and now our own Thought and Mind, is he not vastly mistaken? Does he not altogether destroy god, when he denies that any compound is Imperishable, since it never abides in the same condition, so that he makes any notion of god impossible? For at one moment Democritus says that Images, endowed with divinity, are present in the universe, and then that the first-beginnings of Mind, which are also in the universe, are gods, and then Images endowed with Psyche, which are wont to benefit us or do us harm, and then some Images so huge that they embrace the whole universe from without. ... (43, 120)..." (*FV*, 55 A 74).

"Some have thought that we derived our concept of the gods from the strange things that happen in the universe, and Democritus seems to be of this opinion, for he says that men of old, seeing that which took place in the sky, such as thunder and lightning and bolts of lightning and the conjunctions of stars and eclipses of sun and moon, feared the gods because they supposed that the gods were responsible for these" (*FV*, 55 A 75).

"The air is full of these Images" (*FV*, 55 A 78).

"Democritus represented these Images as entering into human beings and into irrational animals from the Being of God" (*FV*, 55 A 79).

The fact that Leucippus and Democritus are habitually called "Atomists" is responsible for the dense cloud of misunderstanding that has enveloped their doctrines. The Greek word ἄτομος (atom) means "that which cannot be cut into parts," the "indivisible." The Epicurean "atom" is already very different from that of Leucippus; the "atom" of which Gassendi spoke was very different from the Epicurean; and the "atom" of modern science, which is part of the theory of the inner structure of matter, resembles no one of its homonymous predecessors, and in recent physical theory at least is not an atom, since it has ceased to be indivisible. The confusion which has thus been created by the use of the same term to designate a series of different conceptions has been further magnified, ever since the time of Aristotle, by the use of careless and unhistorical expressions on the part of historians of philosophy.

Aristotle, in the course of the hostile survey of previous philosophies which forms the greater part of Book I of the *Metaphysics*, makes the following statement about Leucippus and Democritus: "They say that the Full and the void are the elements, calling the one Being and the other non-being; Being is that which is full and solid,[7] and non-being is that which is empty and rare[7] (wherefore they say that Being is no more truly than non-being is, because void is, but is no more truly than body[8]; and they make these the causes of things that

---

[7] The terms "solid" and "rare" are Aristotelian additions.

[8] Retaining the reading of all the MSS.: ὅτι οὐδὲ τό κενὸν τοῦ σώματος. There is

are as their matter (ὡς ὕλην)." This is to say, Aristotle himself recognizes four causes, substance or essence, matter or substratum, the source of movement or change, and the end or good: and he rejects the system of Leucippus on the ground that Leucippus has recognized only one of these four causes, and says that that one resembles the "material" cause. If it were not for the overpowering authority that Aristotle still exercises over the minds of men, this statement of Aristotle would long ago have been admitted to be an *ex parte* and false criticism, which is not consistent even with Aristotle's own terminology. What did Aristotle mean by matter (ὕλη)?

Aristotle was the first, with one doubtful exception,[9] to use ὕλη in a strictly philosophical sense. If we turn to the excellent definition given by Ross, we find that "matter is not for Aristotle a certain kind of thing, as we speak of matter in opposition to mind." On the contrary, "it is a purely relative term relative to form. . . , the materials of a thing as opposed to the structure that holds them together, the determinable as opposed to the determinant." Now Aristotle did not go quite so far as to say that the Atoms and the void actually were material causes; he merely said that they resembled material causes, or that they were "of the nature of matter" (ἐν ὕλης εἴδει). But even within this limitation, how is it possible to detect any resemblance between the Indivisible Beings of Leucippus, and the part they play in his system, and the formless potential indeterminate matter of Aristotle, and the part it plays in the system of Aristotle? The Indivisible Beings of Leucippus do indeed move, but in every other respect they are at the other pole of thought from matter; they are Eternal, of substance that is forever identical with itself, and they are Immutable; they are the source of all Life and Mind, since they are of the Being of God (θείας οὐσίας). We conclude, therefore, that this statement of Aristotle need not be and should not be

no need to assume that the original text of the *Metaphysics* was always strictly logical.

[9] *Met.*, edited by Ross, I, 128.

taken seriously, any more for example than the remark of Parmenides about the way of investigation "which has been imagined by two-headed mortals who know nothing." Heraclitus was not "blind and deaf and stupefied," simply because Parmenides said that he was; and similarly Leucippus is not a "materialist," simply because Aristotle said that he was.

Let us then suppose that we approach the available evidence about the doctrines of Leucippus and of Democritus with minds free from those prejudgments which have been engendered by subsequent applications of the term "atom" and by the natural vanity of Aristotle. It may be said at once that with the exception of the encyclopaedic tendencies of Democritus, and his creation of a considerable system of ethics, there is little or nothing to distinguish the philosophical attitudes of the two men; and I shall henceforth refer to Leucippus and to Democritus indifferently, with the understanding that Leucippus was the pioneer, and that Democritus agreed with him in every essential doctrine.

In order to understand the Indivisible Beings of Leucippus, we must first recapitulate the attributes of the supreme god of Parmenides. The supreme god of Parmenides was One Being, Indivisible, since "it is all alike," Continuous, Immovable (which means Immutable) since it is "held by mighty Necessity within the bonds of Limit," Perfect because it is Limited, Inviolable since "it lies uniformly within Limits" and is not scattered and divided, "Full of Being throughout," and therefore Full of Thinking and the Cause of Thought, and Limited, so that it is One Spherical Form, the Cause of the form of the universe. What changes was Leucippus forced to make in this supreme god, in order to endow it with a more direct and more obviously causal relation with changing phenomena? It must become plural, without ceasing to be the supreme reality; and Leucippus accordingly made his Indivisible Beings Infinite in number and quantity. Each of these new Beings is very small, "so that it escapes the senses" (*FV*,

55 A 37), and can be "observed only by speculative reason" (*FV*, 55 A 102, 124); but in every other inherent respect, except Form, these new Beings remain identical with the One Being of Parmenides. They are all Indivisible, that is to say they are all Full of continuous and uniform Being; they are all internally Immovable in the sense that they are Immutable. The One Being of Parmenides was a Spherical Form; these new Indivisible Beings are all indeed Forms, but they are not all Spherical Forms, and the explanation of this difference between the two doctrines is of vital importance to the understanding of Leucippus.

We have already seen that Parmenides adopted the attribute of Spherical Form in order to ensure a causal bond between his supreme god and the universe. For the purpose of Parmenides, one Form was enough to express the causal relation between his one god and the one universe. But at this very point, Leucippus has contradicted his master; he has assumed an infinite number of changing universes ($\check{a}\pi\epsilon\iota\rho a$ $\epsilon\hat{i}\nu a\iota$ $\tau\grave{a}$ $\pi\acute{a}\nu\tau a$), and therefore he must assume that the Forms are Infinite in number and quantity. Furthermore, these new Forms are not limited each One to the task of causing the form of a universe; they are the Causes ($a\grave{i}\tau\acute{i}a\iota$) of all phenomena everywhere, the least as well as the greatest; and since Form is the attribute of Being that expresses its divine causal relation to phenomena, and since the diversity of phenomena is infinite, these new Forms must be of infinite variety. Since the Forms are imperceptible, and are accessible only to reason, no one Form is adequate by itself to produce a phenomenon which is by definition perceptible; therefore these Formal Causes must combine in order to produce phenomena. Thus we reach the point at which Leucippus was forced to deal with the problems of motion, change, and non-being.

Since the Forms are Continuous Full Being throughout, and are incapable of internal change or movement, all change and movement and phenomena must depend upon the introduction of some other kind of reality, which must be so conceived as to permit the Forms to exercise their causal power. This other kind of reality may be regarded in two ways; from one point of view, it will be that which separates the Forms and prevents them from coalescing into the Immovable Immutable One Being of Parmenides, and from another point of view it will be the opposite of the Forms. The Forms are Full, but this new reality must be empty of Being; the Forms are Being, and this new reality must be non-being. Once more Leucippus has contradicted his master. Parmenides had denied the reality of non-being; but Leucippus maintains the reality of non-being. If non-being were not a reality, the Infinite and Indivisible Forms would remain as sterile and motionless as the One Being of Parmenides. And this non-being is the void, in contrast to the Full; the term had been originally suggested by Pythagoras, as that which separated his microcosmic phenomena, in each of which the One had been combined in definite proportions with that which was "other." Zeno had used the void, in his arguments against the enemies of the motionless One Being; and Leucippus found the concept ready forged and quite adequate to his purpose. It must not be confused with empty space; the Greeks had not yet invented the notion of a continuous substratum underlying all phenomena. The void, which was also non-being, was merely an interruption of Being, which permitted Beings to move and so to cause phenomena: but it was a necessary interruption.

Once non-being is assumed, motion is possible, and the Forms, Infinite in number and variety, engage in their eternal task of causing phenomena. Aristotle characteristically remarked that Leucippus and Democritus "lazily neglected the cause of movement" (*Met.*, 985 b 19), which merely means that they did not explain it as Aristotle explained it. The motion of the Forms is eternal, and what is eternal of course has no origin or beginning in time; eternal motion simply expresses the eternity of the causal process. As for the details of the process by which a universe is formed, they are tolerably clear in the account given by Diogenes Laertius. The process resembles in general the account given by Anaxagoras; there is a single revolution, which leads to a separation of the Forms, during which "like Forms join like" and the fine Forms, those which constitute Fire and Air, depart toward the outer void "as if sifted out." There is a containing "membrane" which is just outside the orbit of the Sun, and within which the fiery Stars are also formed; this containing membrane is of course the precise equivalent of the containing Air or Pneuma which is so familiar in the system of Anaximenes, and in the system of Anaxagoras.

Among the infinite variety of Forms that create the infinitely various phenomena, one special Form is singled out by Leucippus and Democritus. Their master Parmenides had insisted upon the divine perfection of the One Spherical Form; and now Leucippus and Democritus identify the infinite number of Indivisible Beings that possess Spherical Form with Mind, Psyche, Fire, and God. These divine Spherical Forms are the Panspermia, the mixture of all Seeds, and they are the elements that produce all nature; and incidentally they are also Air and Pneuma, since Psyche is maintained within bodies by the process of respiration, just as it was in the doctrine of Heraclitus. These Spherical Forms, which generate life throughout the universe, are distributed in varying proportions throughout the universe; in ordinary animals they are of course Mind and Psyche, but since they occur everywhere, even in stones, even a stone has Psyche. And the proof of the presence of Psyche in the apparently inanimate, if proof be needed, is the fact that stones come into being, and therefore "there is Psyche in a stone just as in any other Seed which brings anything into being." In the case of ordinary animals, these Spherical Forms are placed "one beside one alternately in pairs" with the Forms, not Spherical, that produce the body of the animal. These Spherical Forms are contrasted with other Forms not only because of their special functions as Mind, Psyche, and God, but also because they possess to a peculiar degree the power of penetrating everything else, and "can most easily move everything else," since "Psyche imparts motion to all living beings." That is to say, all Forms tend to move, but the Forms that produce bodies are expressly contrasted with the Forms that constitute Mind and Psyche; the less subtle Forms tend to "stay together and become entangled," and every such entanglement is a "system," whether large or small. The universe itself is such a system, and is contained within a membrane which consists of the Finer Shapes of Fire and Air, and is in constant revolution; and this revolving membrane dries out the muddy systems that adhere to it, and converts them into divine Fire, and they become the Stars.

If we now turn to the account given of the process of respiration, we shall see that there is a definite analogy between the ordinary animal and the stone, as one descends in the scale of organisms, and between the ordinary animal and the universe, as one ascends that scale. The Spherical Forms that enter into the body of an animal from outside are represented as "keeping in check that which presses upon and solidifies bodies," but when there is no longer strength enough to maintain the process of respiration, the animal "dies," and the Spherical Forms of its Psyche are dispersed. But "death," in the philosophy of Leucippus, is only a relative term; there is no such thing as a body that is absolutely "dead," since even bodies that are called dead partake of something "warm and endowed with sensation, that penetrates the greater part with its Pneuma (Breath)," and since even a stone, which is a "solidified body," has Psyche. On the other hand, as death is but a relative term, so Life is but a relative term; and the Spherical Forms which constitute Fire and Air and Pneuma are the divine source not only of Psyche in the ordinary animals, but of those divine Fires which we call the Stars, and of the Images which "are great and marvellous and almost but not quite Imperishable," of which "some do good and some do evil." The Spherical Forms are therefore endowed, according to Leucippus and Democritus, with the highest degree of causative power. The Spherical Forms are God.

As for the "almost but not quite Imperishable Images," of which some do good and some do evil, it is obvious that they stand for the daimons of traditional Greek belief. Like the lesser gods in the system of Empedocles, they could not be Eternal, since they were combinations of Forms, and no combination of Forms is Eternal, not even that combination which we call the universe. Democritus seems to have distinguished one class of these Images from a superior class whom he expressly called "the gods," who "give all good things to men, but never give what is harmful, useless, or evil"; but even this superior class cannot have been quite Imperishable.

The Spherical Forms themselves, which are the supreme god of Leucippus, stand therefore in precisely the same relation to the other Forms of Being that Heraclitus established between his supreme god Fire and the lower forms of Fire. The Spherical Forms consist throughout of pure Being, and all other Forms consist throughout of pure Being, just as the lower forms of Fire really consisted of Fire; but the highest degree of causal activity is reserved to the Spherical Forms, and the other Forms, despite their identity of Being, are represented as less mobile, and therefore more apt to be entangled in the sort of combinations which are to be found at the centre of the universe. These inferior Forms as they combine constitute "all kinds of bodies," and it should be noted that Leucippus did not regard any Form, even an inferior Form, as a body. Aristotle, who habitually applied technical terms derived from his own philosophy to the concepts of other philosophers, asserted, in the *De Generatione et Corruptione*, 316 b, that the belief in "indivisible bodies and magnitudes" could only be justified on the ground that "there was a limit, beyond which breaking-up could not proceed" without causing the body to perish utterly, which would be an impossible consequence. On the other hand, Aristotle asserted that the belief in "indivisible bodies" must itself be rejected, because it led to a series of consequences which were absurd and impossible, and which he gave in detail in the *De Caelo*, 303, and the *Physics* 231 a 18 *ff*. In other words, Aristotle invented an argument, of which there is no trace in any of the other sources from which we derive our information about Leucippus and Democritus, and which depends for its validity upon the assumption that the Indivisible Beings of Leucippus are "bodies and magnitudes." But "bodies and magnitudes" are Aristotelian technical terms, employed by him to signify respectively "objects made out of sensible, mutable perceptible matter" and "objects that are pure extension" and are made of intelligible matter. These latter are the geometrical objects that are studied by mathematicians. What validity can we justly assign to the assumption that the Indivisible Beings of Leucippus are identical with the divisible, mutable, and transient "bodies and magnitudes" of which Aristotle speaks?

The answer is obvious. The assumption made by Aristotle is completely invalid; it was made by him in order to bolster up, temporarily, an argument that he had himself invented, in order that the collapse of that argument might be the more dramatic and convincing, and in the hope that when the argument collapsed, it would carry with it the systems of Leucippus and of Plato. For the mathematical objects that Aristotle calls "magnitudes" are his version of the physical system of Plato, just as "bodies" are his version of the Indivisible Beings. In fact, the Indivisible Beings are objects of thought, devoid of all sensible quality and substance; and they are not bodies, subject to perception and change, but are themselves the causes of all bodies; they are not magnitudes such as are studied by the mathematician, and necessarily subject to division, but are Imperishable Forms which consist of pure Being, and though they are separated by void, they are not divisible by void or by anything else. If Aristotle had said that there were certain Forms, not Spherical, which moved less rapidly than the Spherical Forms, and tended to constitute such compound bodies as stones and earth, he would have been within the limits of fair criticism. For it is quite true that the perfection of the divine Spherical Forms, as portrayed by Leucippus, carries with it an implied criticism of all other Forms, which are inevitably endowed with a lower degree of causal power, simply because their Forms are other than Spherical. In other words, all Forms are divine, because all Forms consist of the Being of God; but some are lower than others, and the name of God is reserved by Leucippus and Democritus for the Spherical Forms, precisely as Heraclitus identified his supreme god with Fire, and not with the lower forms of Fire.

Unfortunately, the terminology which Aristotle incorrectly applied to the Indivisible Beings, and the false notions which go with the use of such terminology, gained currency for reasons which are obvious to all who have studied the history of Aristotelianism, and who are aware of the extent to which the arguments employed by Aristotle, and the conclusions which Aristotle reached, have dominated the minds of men, not only of "those who know," of professional scholars and theologians, philosophers and scientists, but also indirectly of the multitudes of men who do not know, and are incapable of judging for themselves, and are forced to rely upon the authority of professionals. A little later, I shall return to this question of Aristotle's influence, so far as it concerns the history of the ideas and the thought of the early Greek philosophers; but for the moment an attempt must be made to outline the attitude of Leucippus and Democritus towards the theory of knowledge, and towards science, mechanism, and that vague series of vaguer concepts that is known as materialism.

The Indivisible Forms, that by combining cause bodies that are perceptible to the senses, and the void that separates all Forms and permits them to move either slowly or rapidly, are the only two realities, and consequently the only true knowledge is knowledge of the Forms and the void. This is equivalent to saying that all other knowledge is false; and it will be observed that Democritus included in this implied condemnation all systems of philosophy that do not recognize the Forms and the void, as well as all the knowledge that is derived from the senses, which he expressly called "bastard" knowledge. Phenomena, and the qualities that are perceptible in phenomena, are therefore not the truth; but since they are caused by realities, they may be spoken of as the "criterion for the comprehension of things unseen," and are themselves, like the phenomena in the system of Anaxagoras, not complete unrealities, but are a revelation of the Forms and the void. This must be the excuse for Aristotle, when he says that Democritus "held that the truth *is* that which appears"; it would be difficult to invent a phrase which would more effectively distort the view of Democritus. And yet the statement of Aristotle would be correct, if he had only said that the truth was "in" that which appears.[10] However, since the phenomena perceived by the erring senses are related to the truth, since they are caused by realities, they will when properly regarded by the light of reason afford some true knowledge, not only about phenomena but about the Forms and the void. Our "bastard" knowledge of phenomena teaches us that they undergo unending change, and that they have an apparently infinite variety of sensible qualities; our true knowledge of them teaches us that the apparent changes are limited to phenomena and do not affect the Forms except as they change their position and their arrangement, and that the infinite variety of sensible qualities is in reality a deception produced by the underlying causal realities which never vary, except in position and arrangement, and are altogether devoid of sensible qualities. Void is always non-being; and the Forms are always Being. In this sense Leucippus and Democritus say that "nothing is really of one quality rather than of an-

---

[10] In the passage from the *De Generatione et Corruptione*, 315 b, translated above, Aristotle, having no motive for distorting the doctrine of Leucippus, reported it correctly, and said that the truth was "in the appearance" (ἐν τῷ φαίνεσθαι).

other," where "nothing" refers to any phenomenon or combination of Forms. That is to say, the infinite diversity of phenomena is merely an appearance.

Yet the infinite diversity and the constant change are, so to speak, real appearances; and in order to maintain the causal bond between the Forms and the void, and that which they cause, Leucippus was forced to introduce infinity into the causal realities. Hence the number and quantity of Forms is infinite, precisely as the quantity of Anaximander's Apeiron was infinite, in order "that coming into being and change in things may never cease" (Simplicius, *Phys.*, 28). Why then must Leucippus assume that the variety of Forms is also infinite? Aristotle says that Leucippus and Democritus account for the manner in which things come into being by three things, namely "differences in Form, Turning, and Contact"; two of these differences belong to motion rather than to the Indivisible Being itself, and the one that remains, difference in Form, is the only attribute of the Indivisible Being that serves to distinguish it from other Indivisible Beings, and is therefore the only real source, inherent within the Beings themselves, of the apparent qualitative differences observed in phenomena. This emphasis upon the causal function of Form is therefore an integral part of the system of Leucippus; and both he and his follower seem to have used the terms ῥυσμός and ἰδέα, Form, even more often than the term Indivisible Being ἄτομος οὐσία or φύσις, to refer to the most important attribute of the supreme ultimate reality that they recognized.

The two absolute realities in which Leucippus believed are both metaphysical; Being and the void are beyond the reach of sense-perception, and are accessible only to the operations of true reason, and true reason has only one available source, namely the Spherical Forms which are the supreme god of Leucippus and of Democritus. Of these divine Forms, the Psyche and the Mind of man are composed; and when a man dies, the Spherical Forms that were his Psyche cease to perform their causal function within his body, and are scattered;

but only man's individual and temporary Life is affected by their dispersion, and the Eternal Spherical Forms, wherever they are, continue to be Life and Mind, and to cause the phenomena of Life throughout the universe.

The activity of Leucippus probably did not extend far beyond the task of establishing his metaphysical system; but Democritus seems to have had the wide-ranging curiosity of Aristotle, and applied the system to the explanation of many phenomena. In this limited sense he was a scientist, as were many Greek philosophers before and after his time; but neither he nor Leucippus was a scientist, in the sense in which a scientist is a man ready to abandon any theory or any hypothesis before the evidence of a discordant fact. Leucippus said that "no thing comes into being at random, but all things come from Reason and through the action of Necessity." Does this mean that he was a materialist, or that he believed that the observed phenomena of motion were due to the operation of mechanical laws which could be mathematically stated? Not in the least. If by some miracle the Aristotelian notion of matter could have been explained to Leucippus, assuming that Leucippus had strength of mind enough to retain his own convictions, he would have rejected Aristotelian matter as a false hypothesis; he would have rejected with equal zeal modern notions of matter as something which is contrasted with mind, or as something that is a system of radiations or of waves, or as a structure composed of a more primitive stuff that is neither mental nor material. He had improved upon the Eleatic supreme god by restoring it to full causal activity and a direct relation with phenomena. He had assumed that the Spherical Forms would have the highest degree of causal power; but he never imagined that the Spherical Forms could be regarded as operating mechanically, or in "obedience" to laws external to themselves. The Spherical Forms were themselves divine Reason; and as for the Necessity of which Leucippus speaks, it had from the earliest days of Greek thought been associated with the supreme divine power, not as external to that power but as identical with it or as one of its principal attributes. Leucippus could not foresee that Aristotle would assert that the Forms and the void resembled "material" causes; and he could not foresee that the majority of subsequent philosophers, and of historians of philosophy, would repeat the unfounded assertion of Aristotle.[11]

The Spherical Forms, who were all Thought and Being, were the supreme god of Leucippus. It is now fairly clear that these Forms do not in the least resemble "matter," in either the ancient or the modern acceptations of that term. But it would be well, before taking leave of Leucippus, to clear up this question of matter, and the relation of matter to the philosophy of the Atomists, so far as that can be done in a brief discussion. There is, in the philosophy of the Atomists, a concept that resembles, in its function, Aristotelian matter or ὕλη. That concept is the concept of non-being or the void. The resemblance between these two concepts is far from being an identity, and to establish the limits of the resemblance would require an exposition of the vast system of Aristotle. But it will suffice, for the present purpose, to point out that Aristotle, after Leucippus, recognized the divinity of Form, and that in the hierarchy of Forms the supreme pure Form was the Aristotelian supreme god, and that Aristotle contrasted Form with matter. For Aristotle, the formal cause was very nearly the same as the final cause and as the efficient cause; and the material cause, ὕλη, was that which renders change possible, and which permits locomotion, alteration, change of size, and coming into being and passing away.[12] For Aristotle, matter is that which is expressly contrasted with form. In much the same way, Leucippus employed the con-

---

[11] The doxographers report the doctrine of Leucippus and of Democritus (Diels, *Dox.*, 321, 330) correctly in one passage and incorrectly in another. In 321, Democritean Necessity is, quite correctly, identified with Heimarmene (Destiny), Dike (Justice), and Pronoia (Providence); in 330, which is derived from some hostile critic, the doctrine of a φύσις ἄλογος (substance devoid of reason) is attributed to Leucippus. Under the circumstances, it is fortunate that we have the conclusive evidence of Leucippus himself, which proves that he believed in the supreme causal power of Reason and Necessity.

[12] *Aristotle*, Ross, p. 167.

cept of non-being and void as that which permitted his Indivisible Beings, which were Forms, to move, and thus to
produce all the phenomena of change. If Aristotle had said
that matter, in his system, fulfilled some of the same functions that non-being or void fulfilled in the system of Leucippus, no one could justly have taken exception to the
statement.[13]

We have now reached that period of the fifth century B.C.
when Greek thought, temporarily exhausted and disheartened
by the results of its long effort to attain a perfect definition
of the supreme divine power that governed the universe, left
for a while the battle-ground of metaphysics and of theology,
and sulked in the tents of scepticism. For the first time, men
ventured to proclaim that the ultimate divine reality either
did not exist, or if it did exist, could not possibly be known.
This marks an epoch. There was of course no real breach of
continuity in the Greek effort to know the supreme god; here
and there, in obscurity, the religious ideas of Pythagoras and
his followers were being worked out; and already the inquiry
into the nature of the supreme god, and its relations to the
world and to man, was reviving in the thought of Socrates,
and was to be prolonged in the fiery genius of Plato who rebuilt and extended the religious philosophy of Pythagoras,
in the cold theology and metaphysics of Aristotle, and in the
passionate religious and metaphysical systems of Epicurus
and of Zeno, both of whom resemble a Saint Paul whose
curiosity about this world should not have been quenched by
his certainty of an immediate heaven. Nevertheless, the attitude of the Greek mind was for the moment typified by the
scepticism of brilliant professional men such as Protagoras
and Gorgias, who prepared their young pupils to master the
world of the immediate by means of political skill and the
power of persuasion. The question that Thales and Pythago-

---

[13] The history of metaphysics is of course full of such apparent paradoxes as
this similarity of inner function observable in two concepts, Aristotelian "matter"
and Leucippean "void" or "non-being," that differ greatly in their outer expressions.

ras asked had not received its final answer; it has not yet received a final answer, since finality in this field of investigation is impossible; but the interruption of the sceptics, and the rapid decline of the city-states, that had distracted the minds of men by promising to their privileged citizens a kind of partial and earthly salvation, caused the next wave of inquiry to assume new forms. There is therefore some excuse for treating the history of Greek philosophical thought, down to the time of the sceptics, as a unit.

I have not tried, of course, to deal with the whole history of philosophic thought even during that limited period. At the very outset the inquiry was limited, essentially, to one problem. What transformations did the belief that the substance of the universe was divine undergo during the first great creative period of Greek philosophical thought? The answer given to this question has been incomplete; it is only an approximation to an answer, since a perfect history would so illuminate the available facts that they would become intelligible, so to speak, from the inside, and every utterance of a philosopher would become as clear to us as it would be if we were replaced in his mind and inspired by his purpose. But if we revert to the incomplete answer that has been given, we shall see that the inquiry into the nature of the supreme divine reality has been dominated throughout by certain ideas and convictions that have operated as driving forces, and that have caused the definitions of the supreme god to multiply as one after another has been rejected.

CHAPTER XII

GOD AND THE PHILOSOPHERS

GREEK philosophy set out upon its career under the stimulus of a belief which had been fostered by the poets, and which was shared by the Greek people. This belief held that every power that is manifest in the universe is a god or is divine, that every god is a power, that all gods or divine powers are related to one another, that one god or divine power is supreme over all others, and that there was or had been a cosmogenetic god or divine power from which the actual divine universe and all that is in it, including the other gods, had come into being. The essential novelty of philosophic thought and the feature which differentiates e.g. Thales and Pythagoras from earlier Greeks consists in the fact that Thales and Pythagoras explicitly amalgamated the last two articles of this belief, and identified the cosmogenetic divine power with the supreme divine power. Thales and Pythagoras, moreover, shared the belief of all Greeks that the cosmogenetic power was essentially non-anthropomorphic. But non-anthropomorphic is a merely negative term, and by itself does not explain to us why their thought about the cosmogenetic power took the direction that it did take; it does not explain why one of them named divine Water and the other named divine Fire. We already are aware of the true explanation; their thought automatically took the direction of a substantial part of the actual universe, because all Greeks had for centuries believed that the first gods and the original divine powers were, as a group, identical with the divine substantial universe, and were, as individuals, identical with parts of that universe or with some vague divine power (such as Chaos) out of which that universe grew.

GOD AND THE PHILOSOPHERS

The effort of thought which we call Greek philosophy therefore sprang out of the identification of the supreme god with a divine substance, manifest in the actual universe, and which either produces the universe out of itself (Thales), or produces the universe by combining itself with another substance, which is vague and malleable or, in technical language, "infinite and indeterminate," the ἄπειρον of Pythagoras. It would be impossible to give, in a few words, a summary of the transformations which the doctrines of the supreme cosmogenetic god underwent. But it is possible to discern the fact that there is from the first a kind of dualism[1] expressed or implied, a cleavage between higher and lower forms of the supreme god, or else a cleavage between the perfect substance of the supreme god and the imperfect substance upon which it worked, in every one of these philosophies. This cleavage, this partial dualism, is produced by the conviction, which the philosophers shared with all other Greeks, that the ultimate divine reality is perfect. The belief in the perfection of the supreme god is one of the two great driving forces that stimulated philosophers to differ from their predecessors, to invent new doctrines of the supreme god, and to demolish the theological systems that had hitherto been accepted.

Perfection is a vague term. What one man considers perfect will appear to his friends, to his rivals, and to his successors, imperfect; and the first automatic human expression of the fact that friends, rivals, and successors do not agree with his definition of perfection finds utterance in a denial of his doctrine. Therefore, from the very beginning, philosophers expressed the fact that they disagreed by searching for and choosing new terms that were essentially, or at least to a considerable degree, negative terms. Thus Anaximander contradicted Thales, and at the same time tried to

---

[1] Few terms are more loosely used, in contemporary discussion, than "monism" and "dualism." It is very doubtful whether a genuine monism has ever been held by any philosopher. Those who imagine that they are genuine monists spend a great deal of energy protesting that the phenomena of mind and spirit do not exist, in any real sense: and thus they set up a distinct class of non-being.

invent a more nearly perfect definition of the supreme god, by saying that the supreme god was the Apeiron, the Infinite and Indeterminate divine substance. But it is of the utmost importance, to the understanding of the evolution of philosophy, to notice and to remember that these negations apply in every case only to a part of the preceding doctrine of god or of the universe, and never to the whole of that doctrine. When the supreme god set out upon its career, it was believed by all to be the supreme causal power manifest in the universe, and it was itself, or else the higher forms of it were, the supreme source of life throughout the universe; and the supreme god, although subjected to many a negation, was never entirely stripped of these attributes.

One unifying tendency is discernible in all these negations: it is the tendency to believe that the immutable is more nearly perfect than the mutable. The supreme god was at first either that which changed and was itself all life, or it was that which was the principal source and cause of all change and of all life; but little by little the belief that that which changed or was too closely associated with change must necessarily be imperfect, altered the doctrines of the supreme god; and this tendency culminated in the complete Immutability of the supreme god of Parmenides. Out of the attributes of Life or Psyche, this god retained only Thought, which was the immutable aspect of Mind; out of the attributes of that which exists and changes, this god retained only Being, which is all that is left after change has been subtracted from existence; and out of the attributes of the supreme cause of change, this god retained only Form, which is all that is left after substance has been subtracted from the living body of the universe.

We may also note that these negative terms by which the search for perfection was expressed did not long remain mere negations, and therefore did not long remain practically devoid of significance and of positive meaning; either the philosopher himself, or his successors, proceeded to use these negations as if they were full of positive data, upon which he could construct the rest of his system, or his successors could construct their own denials. Thus terms like Apeiron and Peras, "infinite" and "limit," change their meaning with dizzying rapidity; at one moment the Apeiron will be the perfect supreme god, because Anaximander is contradicting Thales, and at the next moment the Apeiron will be a subordinate, imperfect and passive substance, because Pythagoras is establishing Limit as one of the attributes of his supreme god, the One Fire which limits the apeiron.

The other driving force which operates in Greek philosophical and theological thought is the conviction that the ultimate divine reality must somehow or other account for and explain the universe which is immediately present to the senses. In other words, the causal function is held to be an essential part of the perfection of the supreme god; and from one point of view this force may be regarded as merely an element of the conviction already mentioned, and as one of the aspects of god's perfection. Nevertheless the demand that the supreme god shall be a perfect cause, and that it shall operate in some comprehensible manner to produce the universe, may from another point of view be distinguished from the general quest for perfection. The general quest for perfection had separated the supreme god further and further from that which changes, and had culminated in the theology of Parmenides; but the demand that the supreme god should be a perfect cause and should somehow explain the present universe, tended to plunge the supreme god back into that which changes and to keep it in closer contact with the present universe. This demand generated the theology and the metaphysics of Pythagoras; it generated many of the metaphysical doctrines of all the philosophers, but in particular of Empedocles, Anaxagoras, and Leucippus. And wherever this demand operates, we shall observe that the philosopher who is stimulated by it pays some attention to what is called "science." Only on this one side of his activity does a Greek philosopher ever approach scientific thought; and this side of his activity is always severely and rigidly limited by his own conviction that he must perceive nothing which will mutilate the perfection of his supreme god, and that he must adopt no explanation of phenomena which is inconsistent with that perfection.

Limited as it was by theological or religious beliefs, this side of Greek philosophic activity was the only side on which philosophers made any concession to observable facts, or were willing to proclaim that divine reality could be associated with change. But they spent most of their energy asserting that, after all, change was phenomenal rather than real in the highest sense.

These self-imposed limitations necessarily exercised their influence throughout the history of Greek philosophical thought to hamper the natural curiosity of Greek philosophers, and to obstruct that attention to observed facts which is indispensable to the progress of genuine science, and to the progress of philosophy. The curiosity of the philosophers was not destroyed, and they still paid some attention to facts; but the cosmological theories that they proposed, and their observations of the phenomena of nature, were always conceived and expressed within the limitations of their own special doctrine of the supreme god, in such a manner as to be consistent with the theology and the metaphysics which constituted that part of their philosophy which they believed to be by far the most important.

These two great "driving forces" are of course abstractions from the concrete and individual history of the thought of these philosophers; we must think of them not as external forces, but as human tendencies in which these philosophers shared and to which they yielded. Under their influence, Anaxagoras took the old theology of Anaximenes and brilliantly remoulded it into the doctrine of an infinite divine substance, which could be imagined as infinitely divisible but was really continuous, and of which the highest forms were the one supreme god, which was Air and Aither and Mind. Under their influence, Empedocles invented the notion of the six supreme divine powers which were really the one supreme god of the Sphairos, but which in the illusory intervals between their perfect unity could present all the appearances of change which do, as a matter of fact, interest mortals. Under their influence, Leucippus, a man of rare genius, invented his modification of the One Being of Parmenides, which was motionless Thought and Form, and presented the world with the notion of an infinite number and variety of causal Beings, all of which were Forms, and among which the highest degree of causal power (the functions of Thought and Life) was reserved to his version of the supreme god, to the Spherical Forms which were identical in Being but infinite in number.

These brilliant intellectual inventions all belonged to the realm of theology and metaphysics, and the applications that their own inventors made of them, when they sought to explain by their aid the facts of nature, were as absurd and sterile as one would expect, despite occasional and wholly incidental opinions which strike us as prophetic anticipations of modern scientific knowledge. But, although sterile, so far as science was concerned, at the time when they were originally conceived, they did not remain sterile in the realm of metaphysics. The demonstration of their fertility, and of the metaphysical applications which were made of them by Plato and Aristotle, by Epicurus and Zeno the Stoic, would not here be appropriate; it is enough to notice that the proclamation by Leucippus of the divine causal power of Forms had immense influence over all subsequent thought about the supreme god.

However, the human economy of thought is quite as marvellous as the human economy of labor; and the fact that an intellectual invention, a device or a mechanism of the mind, was originally destined to serve as a metaphysical concept and as an explanation of god, will not forever prevent it from being exploited as a scientific hypothesis and as an explanation of natural phenomena. All that needs to be omitted or suppressed is its divinity, its status as a divine cause, its historical association with Psyche, which is Life and Mind. All this can be easily accomplished, by one who is not reluctant to divest a theological concept, a theory of the supreme god, of its divine perfection, by one who is willing to deaden it and to allow it to sink to a lower level than that on which it is maintained by the faith of its inventor and by those who share that faith. The ease with which a theological concept can be thus transformed, the rapidity with which a definition of the supreme god may be transposed into a definition of a lower form of being, or even into a definition of non-being or of matter, accounts for the fact that the four gods of Empedocles soon became the four elements, and above all, for the fact that the Indivisible Forms were to Aristotle mere bodies, and that in the seventeenth century they became the corpuscles or atoms which were the material principle in the system of Gassendi, and that later they became the indestructible matter of chemical theory.[2]

Even in the eyes of Aristotle, the Indivisible Forms of Leucippus had already lost their divinity and their life, and had become bodies. Does this mean that the view of Aristotle represents the historical truth about the thought of Leucippus? On the contrary, it means merely that Aristotle had invented his own doctrine of the supreme god and his own metaphysical system, and that consequently he had lost faith in all metaphysical doctrines which had been invented by anyone else, and which consequently appeared to him in an alien and a hostile light. He therefore did not take the trouble to try to understand them, when he was discussing the ultimate divine reality, i.e. metaphysics, the supreme god. When Aristotle was treating of physical doctrines, he referred politely to Leucippus and to Democritus; his attitude was no longer hostile, because he was willing to allow that other

[2] Thus the "atoms" always managed to retain the reality which they had originally in the system of Leucippus, although they had lost the rest of their divine attributes by modern times.

philosophers had made some genuine contributions to the explanation of phenomena and of nature, as distinguished from the supreme god. To be sure, he owed an incalculable debt to the Greek theologians who had preceded him; but he was not aware of that fact, and found it easy to represent them all, with the exception of Anaxagoras, as men "who spoke at random" on the topic of the supreme god, and who were incapable of making the correct use of the causes that they had discovered. Since he believed in his own version of the supreme god, he did not believe in theirs; and the divine substances, which had been the supreme gods of most of the earlier thinkers, promptly sank to the low status of mere "material causes," and the long effort to endow each of those gods with every imaginable perfection, on which some of the greatest Greek minds had liberally expended their genius, appeared to Aristotle to be random talk.

The demonstration that Aristotle thus gave of his own lack of gratitude to his great predecessors, and of the fact that he did not understand their doctrines of the supreme god, does not in the least, of course, indicate that he himself was not a great genius. But it does prove that for certain definite reasons, and because he worshipped exclusively his own vision of the ultimate divine reality, he became incapable of seeing the effort furnished by philosophers as one continuous effort, impeded by lack of knowledge and by all manner of human failings, to deepen and to intensify our understanding of reality. And since he was incapable of seeing the search for reality as a continuous effort, he was also incapable of taking warning from the partial failure of his predecessors, and insisted upon expanding his own contribution to the common thought of mankind into one more system. For surely systems of philosophical thought err in many ways, but perhaps most of all by being nominally, and in the conceit of their makers, complete, finished, irremediable. Since their makers aim at completeness, they are wilfully blind to some part of those truths which others have already made available; and they generate the war of philosophical sects, in which finally all systems perish, not only because their dead bulk is out of all proportion to their living content, but because new, although still partial, truths are discovered.

Aristotle is not at all more guilty, in respect of this failure to see and to judge his predecessors truly, than many another great philosopher; and his name has been mentioned in this connection only because his interpretation of early Greek philosophy has been long accepted, and widely accepted, without due examination of the basis upon which it rests. Nor are similar failures confined to philosophers. Nothing is more easy than to fall into the habit of surveying both the language used by others, and the thought that they intend to convey by that language, from the outside, and of estimating the merits and the demerits of their thought entirely by its external appearance. In order to understand others, an effort is required; we must momentarily abandon our egotism, and few things, perhaps, are more difficult. Within the brief period of the sixth and fifth centuries B.C., one philosopher after another denounced the theological doctrines of his predecessors, with varying degrees of violence. Pythagoras and Xenophanes denounced the theology of Homer and Hesiod; Heraclitus denounced the theologies of Hesiod, Pythagoras, Xenophanes, and Hecataeus; Parmenides repaid Heraclitus by calling him blind, deaf, dumb, and ignorant; and Empedocles referred to the Eleatics as madmen and fools. Even those philosophers who did not, so far as we know, resort to violent abuse of the theology of their predecessors, expended much of their mental energy in contradicting that theology, with the inevitable result, as we have seen, that each new doctrine of the supreme god has been expressed, to a considerable extent, in negative terms.

Because this tendency is universal, the fact that this or that particular philosopher occasionally misrepresented the doctrines of his predecessors is comparatively trivial. Some degree of misrepresentation is inevitable, whenever one human being undertakes to report the thought of another human being. But the really important fact is that each of these philosophers misunderstood the thought of his predecessors, and that, because he more or less misunderstood, he felt free to deny, to contradict, and to abuse (in the worst cases) their doctrines of the ultimate divine reality, without having first submitted himself to the most severe of all intellectual disciplines. There is nothing mysterious about the nature and essence of this discipline; it is the discipline of the history of philosophy, and it consists in making the effort which is necessary in order to understand the thought and the expression of others, and in prolonging that effort until some degree of success has been attained. Without this discipline, the practice of philosophical thought does not indeed become impossible; that has been demonstrated by the brilliant achievement of the period that we have been studying, and in fact by the achievements of philosophers in all subsequent periods. But the fact that this discipline has been neglected, not only by fifth century Greeks, but ever since, accounts, in great measure, for the destructive and irrational warfare carried on by philosophical schools and sects, and for the fact that the history of philosophy resembles the history of a series of retreats from untenable positions, rather than the progressive conquest of a more complete understanding of ultimate reality.

Beneath the negations and contradictions, in which some even of the greatest philosophers have felt themselves compelled to express their thought, there lies the small but infinitely precious portion of living truth, of genuine intuition, that it is the privilege of genius to contribute to philosophy. Philosophy cannot be successful, and its effort cannot be continuous and genuinely progressive, like the effort of the physical sciences, unless philosophers are able and are willing to submit themselves to the discipline of the history of philosophy. The discipline of the history of philosophy, when it is fully understood, is much more rigorous, and makes greater demands upon the mind, than the discipline of the physical sciences, for the plain reason that it is more difficult to understand the real meaning of the thought of other human beings, and to understand living reality, than it is to comprehend the relations between phenomena that are studied by the physical sciences.

In so far as philosophers refuse to submit themselves to this discipline, they sever themselves, deliberately or involuntarily, from all that is living and is valid in the thought and the philosophical achievements of other men; and behind the barricade of their own arrogance they will continue to build, upon the ruins of other systems, new systems. So Heraclitus built upon the ruins of the theology of Xenophanes; so Parmenides built upon the ruins of Heraclitus. Furthermore, it is clear that this discipline cannot be imparted by books, since the effort which such discipline requires is in the nature of the case personal, and cannot be performed vicariously. Philosophy does not neglect or scorn the realities with which physical science deals; but the methods and the discipline of philosophy must necessarily be different, since philosophy, in its origin and even now, must attempt to deal with the reality of life itself. If the discipline of the history of philosophy comes to be more widely practised, it is possible that philosophic thought will gradually release itself from its present servitude to science, and will take up problems one by one, and will reach solutions capable, as are the solutions reached by science, of continual improvement, and which contain a growing portion of truth.

SELECT BIBLIOGRAPHY

Allen, T. W., *The Homeric Catalogue of Ships.* Oxford, 1921.
  Homer; the Origins and the Transmission. Oxford, 1924.
Bérard, V., *Les Phéniciens et l'Odyssée.* Paris, 1902.
Blass, F., *Die Interpolationen in der Odyssee.* Halle, 1904.
Drerup, E., *Homerische Poetik.* I *Das Homerproblem in der Gegenwart.* Würzburg, 1921.
Finsler, G., *Homer.*[3] Leipzig, 1924.
Lang, A., *Homer and His Age.* London, 1906.
Laurand, L., *Progrès et recul de la critique.* Paris, 1913.
Leaf, W., *Troy.* London, 1912.
  Homer and History. London, 1915.
Mülder, D., *Die Ilias und ihre Quellen.* Berlin, 1910.
Murray, G., *The Rise of the Greek Epic.*[3] Oxford, 1924.
Rothe, C., *Die Ilias als Dichtung.* Paderborn, 1910.
  Die Odyssee als Dichtung. Paderborn, 1911.
Scott, J. A., *The Unity of Homer.* Berkeley, 1921.
Shewan, A., *The Lay of Dolon.* 1911.

HESIOD

Mazon, P., *Les Travaux et les Jours.* Paris, 1914.
  Hésiode. Paris, 1928.
Powell, J. U., *New Chapters in the History of Greek Literature,* Second Series (Appendix I, pp. 198 *ff.*). Oxford, 1929.
Séchan, L., "Pandora," *Bulletin de l'Association Guillaume Budé,* Avril, 1929, pp. 3-36.

GREEK RELIGION

Adam, J., *The Religious Teachers of Greece.*[2] Edinburgh, 1909.
Boulanger, A., *Orphée.* Paris, 1925.

Cornford, F. C., *From Religion to Philosophy*. London, 1912.
Greek Religious Thought from Homer to the Age of Alexander. London, 1923.

Farnell, L. R., *The Cults of the Greek States*. Oxford, 1896-1909.
Greek Hero Cults and Ideas of Immortality. Oxford, 1921.
Outline History of Greek Religion. London, 1920.

Gruppe, O., *Griechische Mythologie und Religionsgeschichte*. Leipzig, 1908.

Kern, O., *Die Religion der Griechen*, I. Berlin, 1926.
Die griechischen Mysterien. Berlin, 1927.
Orphicorum fragmenta. Berlin, 1922.

Moore, George Foot, *History of Religions*, I. New York, 1916.

Murray, G., *Five Stages of Greek Religion*. New York, 1925.

Nägelsbach, C. F., *Homerische Theologie*.[3] Nürnberg, 1884.

Nilsson, M. P., *History of Greek Religion*. Oxford, 1925.
The Minoan-Mycenaean Religion. Lund, 1927.

Pettazzoni, R., *La religione nella Grecia antiqua*. Bologna, 1921.
I Misteri. Bologna, 1923.

Rohde, E., *Psyche* (English translation from the 8th edition). New York, 1925.

Rose, H. J., *Primitive Culture in Greece*. London, 1925.

Greek Philosophy

Aristotle, *Metaphysics*. Text, introduction and commentary by W. D. Ross. Oxford, 1924.

Bailey, C., *The Greek Atomists and Epicurus*. Oxford, 1928.

Bodrero, E., *Eraclito*. Torino, 1912.

Bréhier, E., *Histoire de la pholosophie*, I. Paris, 1926.

Burnet, J., *Early Greek Philosophy*.[3] London, 1920.
Greek Philosophy, Part I. London, 1914.

Bywater, I., *Heracliti reliquiae*. Oxford, 1877.

Carcopino, J., *La basilique pythagoricienne de la Porte Majeure*. Paris, 1926.

BIBLIOGRAPHY

Commentaria in Aristotelem graeca. Berlin, 1882.

Decharme, P., *La critique des traditions religieuses chez les Grecs.* Paris, 1904.

Delatte, A., *Études sur la littérature pythagoricienne.* Paris, 1915.
    La vie de Pythagore de Diogène Laërce. Bruxelles, 1922.
    Essai sur la politique pythagoricienne. Liège, 1922.

Diels, H., *Doxographi Graeci.* Berlin, 1879.
    Die Fragmente der Vorsokratiker.[3] Berlin, 1912. (Referred to as *FV*.)

Diès, A., *Le cycle mystique.* Paris, 1909.

Gianola, A., *La fortuna di Pitagora presso i Romani.* Catania, 1921.

Gilbert, O., *Griechische Religionsphilosophie.* Leipzig, 1911.

Krische, A. B., *Die theologischen Lehren der griechischen Denker.* Göttingen, 1840.

Macchioro, V., *Eraclito.* Bari, 1922.

Méautis, G., *Recherches sur le Pythagorisme.* Neuchâtel, 1922.

Nock, A. D., *Sallustius. Concerning the gods and the universe.* Cambridge, 1926.

Rivaud, A., *Le problème du devenir et la notion de la matière.* Paris, 1906.

Robin, L., *La pensée grecque.* Paris, 1923. *Tr: Greek Thought*

Ross, W. D., *Aristotle.* London, 1923.

Rostagni, A., *Il verbo di Pitagora.* Torino, 1924.

Scoon, R., *Greek Philosophy before Plato.* Princeton, 1928.

Tannery, P., *Pour l'histoire de la science hellène.* Paris, 1887.

Theophrastus, *Metaphysics.* Translation, commentary, and introduction by W. D. Ross and F. H. Fobes. Oxford, 1929.

Ueberweg-Praechter, *Die Philosophie des Altertums.*[12] Berlin, 1926. (Especially valuable for its bibliography.)

Zeller, E., *Die Philosophie der Griechen.* Erster Teil: Erste Hälfte[7]; Zweite Hälfte.[6] Leipzig, 1920, 1923. *Tr*

INDEX OF NAMES

INDEX OF SUBJECTS